MURDER INC.

MYSTERIES OF THE MOB'S MOST DEADLY HIT SQUAD

BY
CHRISTIAN CIPOLLINI

Table of Contents

80 ෦ 03

THE MURDER INC.

Acknowledgments

Natasha, Kylie, Dirty Harold, Jennifer, Ingrid, Mom, Alex, Jean, Vince, Debbie, Gary. All my wonderful furry pals who are always there for me.

And my entire extended families and friends, all of you have been the greatest support and love I could ever imagined! You are why I do this.

My peers, mentors, colleagues and all those who so generously offered their insight, commentary and advice: MayCay Beeler, Arthur Nash, Joaquin "Jack" Garcia, Ronald Fino, Seth Ferranti, Gerald Posner, Thomas Hunt, Michael Gourdine, Joe Bruno, Pete Forcelli, Scott Deitche, Scott M. Burnstein, John Grenke, Mafialife Chris, Chris Jones, Uffner Family Source.

Ellen Sexton and Lloyd Sealy Library, John Jay College of Criminal Justice

The staff of Strategic Media Books

ઠ ૪૦

Intro:

Lights Out

July 10, 1931

Returning to their home territory of Brownsville at around 9:00 pm, racketeers Irving and Meyer Shapiro had determined it was a good time to decompress. The brothers, along with their associate Jacob "Smokey" Epstein, had spent the day in upstate New York attending another gangster's trial. They decided to then enjoy some games of chance, joining others at the Century Democratic Club where they played cards for hours. As the evening turned into the early morning of July 11, Meyer told the boys they were all going to visit their usual place for final relaxation - the Turkish bath house on Cleveland Street. Meyer, though younger, was considered around town to be "the boss" and therefore both Irving and Smokey were quick to oblige. They reached the bath house, but

Irving suggested Meyer be dropped off first; they would return for him later. The older Shapiro further explained he simply needed to go home and change his underwear. Meyer sent the pair on their way. The return trip was, however, not in Irving's destiny.

Epstein delivered Irving to the apartment building at 691 Blake Avenue in Brooklyn, home to the entire Shapiro family. It was to be a quick clothing change, so the driver remained in the car. But when Shapiro entered the building - something was wrong. The hallway light bulb was out, physically missing. Odd perhaps, but really this was more of an inconvenience, particularly in the darkness of 3:30 am. Shapiro pondered the situation briefly before moving on down the hall. That pause was fatal.

As two gun-wielding shadows descended upon Irving Shapiro, there was no time to react. A dozen shots rang out – nine slugs entered the target's body. The planned attack provided a scene of bloody carnage, and unbeknownst to the killers - a single witness. The mysterious slayers fled on foot to a vehicle, where at least three other covert characters were waiting. Smokey Epstein heard the gunfire and observed two hatless men sprinting from the apartment building. Obviously this was something very bad, so Smoky ran from his car and to the aid of his friend. The effort was in vain; Irving was quite dead.

ॐ ৪০

Chapter 1

Why Kill?

The very first point to be made within the pages of this book – the mob was NOT designed, created, organized, nor operated for the purpose of *killing*. The mob served one purpose… to make money, illicit or legitimate, hand over fist. That's it. So ends the first lesson in organized crime economics. The mob existed to make money.

So then, why is organized crime so ingrained into our minds as a brutal, head busting, murdering machine?

Beyond the many other criminal exploits these gangsters purveyed, at society's expense of course, the bloodlust is what really scares, fascinates and engrosses the culture. There is no cut and dry, simplistic way to answer that. However, suffice to say the mob did kill – a lot sometimes – because such actions were deemed necessary for the purpose of continuing the criminal enterprise. It was a necessity born from an ideology of greed, power and certainly persuasion. Oh yes... the fear of reprisal was, or so the bosses thought, a good psychological device to keep business in order.

The division of gangster brethren this book engages in – the infamously dubbed *Murder Incorporated* – was not formed much differently than any department of legitimate corporate business. Just like legally operating corporate America (okay, the term *legally* is arguable in and of itself, too!), the mob had accounts payable, accounts receivable, public relations, security, a hierarchy of management, logistics... you name it – they employed people or entire crews to handle such industry requirements. However, the mob also had an enforcement arm; a self-policing unit of cold blooded hoods working exclusively under contract for specific upper management entities. Their duty? To keep the business of making money on a smooth road, free of human obstacles that could jeopardize profit making. In the psyche of gangland minds, well, it was all a matter of basic economics. Instilling that fear and carrying out that promise of reprisal was a basic requirement for criminal operations to ensure rules were followed, monetary gain commenced and the bosses would be protected.

How does one go about "jeopardizing" the mob's profits? Many ways actually, but the primary reasons to be paid a visit by the enforcement arm would include: muscling in on another's territory, not paying taxes to the Syndicate, stealing from them, not obeying orders, knowing too much, and of course the ultimate liability which goes hand in hand with "knowing too much" – turning informant. The most brutal of punishments were generally reserved for anyone thought or known to be even remotely considering speaking of the mob's activity to law enforcement. *Rats, stool pigeons, snitches* or *canaries...* all unaffectionate and lethal terms to be branded with. Once labeled as such, the boys from the enforcement regime tagged you with another pair of names: *bum* and *mark*. Neither of those was good to have; both meant you were probably going to die, and it would be a death that served a dual purpose. Particularly gory and tortuous murders were used to both punish the "mark" and to send a very clear message to any and all others who were considering violating mob rules. At first, the death sentences were issued carefully, albeit not entirely laden with solid evidence, but rarely without consideration and certainly always with upper management's sanction. Eliminating other gangland souls, undesirables who were willing participants in the underworld culture of lying, cheating, stealing and of course – killing. The underworld carried out justice within its own microcosm, and all willing players of this seedy game knew the risks.

Another point to be made clear regards the use of two words: mob and mafia. Though far too often used synonymously and interchanged without second thought, these are not the same thing. Well, they were *not exactly* the same entity during the period of time this book delves into. Quite simply... when the rising stars of the New York crime drama actually reached their pinnacle shining moment (1931) – an evolution occurred within an already established concept – multi-ethnic cooperation. Theirs was an organization formed with a *unity* of Italian and Jewish members. Though sometimes credited to men like Charles "Lucky" Luciano, Louis "Lepke" Buchalter, Meyer Lansky, Frank Costello and Benjamin "Bugsy" Siegel, the momentum of inevitable change was more likely learned from their criminal mastermind mentor - Arnold Rothstein. A unified force, they understood, could make far more money than the stringent old school mafia system was ever able to.

However, there is ebb and flow, constant change, growth, birth, death, destruction and rebuilding. So too was the case with the further development of what we call the American Mafia. The truly cohesive mob years peaked for only a decade really. The full formation of five major Mafia families (Sicilian-American blooded membership requirement, for the most part) had also been in development since the bloody *Castellammarese War* was waged between Joe "The Boss" Masseria and Salvatore Maranzano (the war ended in 1931 with the deaths of both men, courtesy of Luciano and his Italian-Jewish alliance). Although some have argued the mafia did not utilize Murder Inc., history shows there were liaisons for and relationships with the direct bosses of the Jewish/Italian murder Syndicate.

The structure of the nation's organized crime system was overdue for change and evolution, but one factor was a solid constant – that need for enforcement. A quote, long attributed to Benjamin "Bugsy" Siegel, sums up how the mob itself perceived the actions of a murder-for-hire department - *"We only kill each other."* So, in a twisted sense – these on-call enforcers were the *instruments of karma*. But as we all know, and can never deny with a straight face, their crimes are never without some form of collateral damage, to the innocent, to the law abiding, to the families, to society, culture and economics as a whole.

What kind of people become killers? A more applicable question is "What kind of people become killers for, at times, a mere five bucks?"

We may never know all the reasons, triggers or motivations; each of Murder Inc.'s members were unique, just as the rest of society is full of individuals each with their own inner motivations in life. That said though, the men chosen for such a demanding occupation had to be the best in their field and positively devoid of any mercy. New York's reigning hot shots of racketeering knew who the most reliable and ambitious recruits were, and for a time - they could be found in Brooklyn.

With that in mind, take a journey into a decade of decadence, fear, violence, sex, life and death of high underworld drama. We will begin with some overview, then venture into a few of the more fascinating individuals, throw in a bunch of irresistibly sinister facts, and maybe even gain some insight into the collective minds of madness we know as Murder Incorporated.

THE MURDER INC.

☙ ❧

Chapter 2:

1931 - The Year of Living Dangerously

Irving's murder was certainly not the first, nor the last acts of brutality involving the Shapiro brothers. Their well-known incivility and sadism was challenged by even more ambitiously cruel and violent enemies. An ongoing war was rapidly escalating into the realm of unconscionable acts of reprisal. The back and forth battles in their case was just a sliver of the larger underworld upheaval going on. Proof that New York's underworld culture was certainly not very organized, certainly revenge-driven, and basically up for grabs was evident in headlines almost every day.

Jack "Legs" Diamond, who was basically a folk hero by that time, was at odds with former allies and competitors both in the city and upstate New York – Shapiros among them. Another notorious set of brothers – the Ambergs - were fighting the Shapiros for slot machine territory in Brooklyn. The most pivotal conflict of all – the *Castellammarese War* – waged between Joe "The Boss" Masseria and Salvatore Maranzano came to an end on April 15th with the assassination of Masseria. His defectors, Charles "Lucky" Luciano leading the dissent, choreographed the kill, and then moved to officially put the old school mob mentality into a final resting place by murdering new boss, Maranzano, on September 10, 1931.

Earning a Place in History

Throughout the chaos of well-known and publicized mob warfare, others were learning lessons, gaining their own reputations and cementing future positions in what was becoming a new crime empire. They were young, most in their early twenties, but already hardened criminals. Brooklyn's toughest, most rebellious and motivated Jewish and Italian hoods were joined up; a mirror image of what occurred with the big boys of mob power in greater New York. They would soon become the ire of law enforcement and judges, the role models for even younger kids growing up in the slums, and known by memorable nicknames like *Happy, Kid Twist, Dasher, Buggsy* and *Pittsburgh Phil.* But most of all... they would prove to be the epitome of organized crime's worst enemy – *itself.*

July 19, 1931...

Three o'clock am, quiet in Brooklyn. Meyer Shapiro and three of his goons had just left a card game. Tired and hungry, they were heading down Church Street for a nearby restaurant when the crack of gunfire erupted. From a trio of snipers - a barrage of a 12 gauge and .38 caliber slugs wildly sprayed the vicinity. Meyer was under attack for the eighteenth time. This attempt on his life was partially expected though. Not even two weeks had passed since his older brother Irving was gunned down at their family home. Police and newspapers reported the intended target was Meyer all along. Still, the younger Shapiro – a boastful boss of Brownsville – had survived yet again. Amazingly, none of the quartet was seriously injured.

The ruckus certainly stirred up the neighborhood though, and to the particular misfortune of the would-be assassins – grabbed the attention of Patrolman Harry Schreck. So instead of finishing their target off and being able to gloat in a job well done, Abe Reles, Harry Strauss and Frank Abbandando found themselves under attack as well. Speeding away from the scene in a stolen Buick, the culprits were recognized by Schreck (Reles gang members were very familiar faces in and around Brooklyn) who then gave chase. Several more officers and detectives joined the patrolman for what became a two-mile pursuit. Police fired no less than thirty shots at the fleeing Buick; the occupants tossing their weapon stash and ammo out the windows. The chase finally ended on Livonia and Howard avenues when the perpetrator-driven car crashed on a sidewalk.

Before the trio could make another effort to escape, the descending cops delivered a few subduing blows with the butts of their revolvers. Reles, Strauss and Abbandando were dragged off to police headquarters for questioning regarding the attempt on Meyer *and* the murder of Irving. All three vehemently denied any knowledge of either crime. So bold were these young men, able to lie and argue before nearly irrefutable evidence. The following morning in court, Reles, stone-faced and unwavering, told the Magistrate he and his companions were simply standing on the sidewalk when police assaulted them.

Why so audacious? These men had history to support their collective prediction of little or no substantial penal repercussions. That customary sequence of *arrest, bail, release, charges dismissed* continued unhampered. For example -

September 10, 1931...

Supreme Court Justice Lewis Fawcett was livid. His disgust did not stem from waking up on the wrong side of the bed on that Thursday morning, but rather from endlessly enduring a proverbial thorn in the side of New York's sense of law and order. The irritation of said thorn had been causing society a festering infection since the days of prohibition. Underworld types consistently marching in and out of courtrooms with little or no debt paid to society. Enough was enough, and then walks in four brazen bad boys, smirking all the way. This was the second time in week he would endure the quartet of twenty-somethings who together tallied almost a hundred arrests already in their young lifetimes. Collectively, these four men were more familiar with handcuffs, chains and leg shackles than most beat cops.

Accompanied by their attorney John J. Riordan, Harry Maione, Harry Strauss, Abraham Reles and Martin Goldstein stood before the judge. Each defendant oozed with a palpable aura of cockiness.

Having been held without bail for violation of the Sullivan Act (1911 law requiring a license for owning and carrying concealable weapons), the men were hoping for some further judicial relief in Fawcett's courtroom. They had been arraigned on a robbery charge only days earlier by a magistrate; the only witness to the alleged crime could not identify any of the alleged culprits. Justice Fawcett ruled for their release. Seemed like a quick exit for the men, or was it?

Detectives had an ace up the sleeve. A statute (really it was a piggy back to disorderly conduct), enabled police to "round up" known criminals that were "consorting" together. Under that law, the presumed bad guys could be held up to one-hundred days. The idea was to then nail them for vagrancy.

When the defendants first appeared in front of Judge Fawcett, they were on considerably stable legal ground. But for good measure, their lawyer pulled the sympathy card. "Observe that they have no marks on them now," warned Riordan, "because they may have as soon as they are rearrested." The implication of possible police brutality was noted by Fawcett, but he had no intention of ruling on anything but his interpretation of the law, which was in the defendants' collective favor.

But... before the men left custody, detectives had taken every key found in their possession and an extensive search began. It was a mission to unlock every door they could find at every address the investigators could think of. Eventually, one key opened the metaphorical Pandora's Box. A Turkish bathhouse on Cleveland Street in Brooklyn housed a locker. Inside that locker? A sawn-off shotgun, six loaded revolvers and a large cache of ammunition. Who originally held the key? Martin Goldstein.

Maione, Strauss, Reles and Goldstein were known to frequent the establishment; many recognized mobsters did. Furthermore, all four of these guys often, upon numerous arrests, gave the bath house as their home address. And so commonly did they visit the bathhouse that cops knew the men would probably return, and in short order. They were right. As predicted, all four young men returned to 602 Cleveland Street. Detectives quickly returned them to magistrate's court. Back to jail they went, yes, but not without their enterprising lawyer right behind them – ready for legal warfare. Although the controversial consorting together statute was being implemented quite a bit in New York that year, not every judge was confident in its constitutionality and some were concerned it was being abused. Furthermore, reputation, prior records and the judge's own perception were not enough to take them off the street without a chance for bail. Police and the magistrate felt, however, the Sullivan violation would suffice. That is why attorney Riordan sought release for his clients in the courtroom of Justice Fawcett yet again.

Still, the judge could not contain his displeasure in New York's lack of allowable punishments for such offenders. Powered by his view of how the outrageous growth of underworld control, and worse yet – the gangsters frequently walking conviction-free out of every courtroom – this would be the twice in one week for his courtroom alone. Fawcett could hold back no more.

His displeasure was clear in warning Riordan, "Persons who possess so many guns are potential murderers."

Although Justice Fawcett thoroughly believed the defendants were guilty as sin even the first time he faced them, a writ of habeas corpus guaranteed them the right to bail. Riordan then argued for considerably low bail with respect to all his clients that day, yet acknowledged that Goldstein was the only member of the foursome he could see possibly getting stiff bail.

Fawcett made a decision. He issued Maione, Reles and Goldstein each $7500 bail, and Strauss $3500, but not without sharp warning.

"We should have here the whipping post and the lash," he declared. "The latter vigorously applied. If we had, they would not come back for a second dose."

The judge further explained his theory was proven in England, Maryland and Delaware, where second offenses occurred far less than in New York. In spite of his verbally expressed belief in a "vigorously applied" lashing of "gangsters and racketeers" – he back peddled adding, "Mind you, I am not advocating that the police beat these men."

Maione, Reles, Strauss and Goldstein strutted out of yet another legal entanglement. Good legal teams, purchased politicians, and a network of gangland hierarchy looking out for them... all the ingredients for a powerful, arrogance inducing potion. Leaving police custody once again, the team was set to dispose of Meyer Shapiro once and for all. Elimination of the Shapiros was both business and personal, especially for Abe Reles. For those emerging as victors... career paths were finalized; professional killers like the world had never imagined.

Only a month after the Reles gang was arrested under the controversial consorting statute, a meeting of uppermost racketeers would commence, birthing – at least partially some believe – the official unification of Italian and Jewish gangsters in a new "Syndicate" of crime and the inauguration of what would become infamously known as *Murder Inc.* Nine Jewish mobsters were arrested at the Hotel Franconia in Manhattan (owned by the late Arnold Rothstein (mentor to several of the men arrested). They were: Joseph "Doc Stacher" Rosen, Benjamin "Bugsy" Siegel, Henry (Harry) Teitelbaum, Louis "Lepke" Buchalter, Harry Greenberg, Louis Kravitz, Jacob "Gurrah" Shapiro, Philip Kovalich and Hyman Holtz. Detectives raided the room based on the same statute that was intended to hold the Reles gang. In similar fashion though, all nine men were eventually released, as the presiding judge felt the law did not justify arresting the men when no criminal act had taken place (though he made a point to express his personal belief most of the men were indeed gangsters). Gangland lore *suggests* the meeting was led by Benjamin "Bugsy" Siegel and Louis "Lepke" Buchalter, possibly at the behest of Meyer Lansky. Besides discussing various rackets they were all involved in, the word was to be spread of a new joint venture with Charles "Lucky" Luciano and his Italian loyalists. Basis for that possibility stems from the general consensus that two assassinations – that of mob bosses Joe "The Boss" Masseria and Salvatore Maranzano – were planned by Luciano and Lansky, carried out by both Italian and Jewish gunmen earlier in 1931.

The gang successfully dispatched Meyer Shapiro into spirit world just two weeks after being released by Justice Fawcett. Meyer's body was discovered in a tenement building on September 17; bullet wound to the head. Reles, Maione, Goldstein, Strauss and Anthony "Tony the Sheik" Carillo were arrested for the murder, but again – all men were soon released. A third Shapiro, Willie, was murdered in 1934.

Meyer Shapiro was presumed responsible for an attempted hit on Reles in 1930. The drive-by shooting injured Martin Goldstein, lodged two .45 caliber slugs into Reles' back and killed George DeFeo. Meyer was also reputed to have kidnapped, battered and raped Abe Reles' sweetheart (who later became his wife) as a message.

On a larger scale, the notoriety Reles and company garnered from their ambition, success and propensity for violent resolve had earned admiration from Louis "Lepke" Buchalter and Jacob "Gurrah" Shapiro (not related to the Shapiro brothers) – two of the major mob figures in competition with both the Shapiro and Amberg brothers (Joe and Louis Amberg's fate came in 1935). Reles, Maione, Strauss and Goldstein had essentially solidified a new career path in the eyes of Lepke. These guys would be the foundation and privileged members of the national Syndicate's *enforcement division*, directly overseen Lepke himself.

ය ෨

Chapter 3

What's in a Name?

Murder Incorporated. Catchy name for a bunch of hired killers, isn't it? So where did such a clever, sinister and aptly-dubbed moniker originate? While there will probably always be some conjecture and debate, the most widely-accepted version gives credit to a reporter from the *New York World Telegram*. Harry Feeney, if he indeed did coin the phrase *Murder Inc.*, was right on target with this one. To dub the group as such was fitting, and considering just how sensationalized the newspapers were (is the news really that different today?) – *memorable*. The name stuck in the minds of law enforcement and the general public, remaining even today as how this branch of the mob is addressed.

And to be fair... the methods by which many of Murder Inc.'s members carried out death sentences was, quite frankly, very worthy of the media's sensationalistic preference anyway. These particular gangsters were rarely recognized for quietly and quickly putting a bullet in a target's head, although that was, of course, a measure sometimes taken. Graduating from the use of hit-and-run gunfire, some of these guys regressed into barbarism. They took great joy in their duty, utilizing extreme brutality with ice picks, rope, meat cleavers, guns, and even fire axes. There has been no collective in organized crime history quite like the murder consortium this book addresses.

However, prior to Feeney's catchphrase taking America by storm (and there is some debate over who really did coin the expression, but we'll get to that shortly) the microcosm of organized crime these killers were part of was referred to as a *"Combination," "Cut-Rate Murder Syndicate"* and *"Murder-for-profit Syndicate."* Being that most of the killers hailed from the Brownsville and Ocean Hill areas of Brooklyn, *"Brownsville Boys"* and the *"Brownsville/Ocean Hill Combination"* were also terms used to distinguish them. The word "Combination" was apparently how the killers themselves referred to the group, according to one its own top ranking members – Abe "Kid Twist" Reles. *Combination* had been commonly employed by the press and law enforcement alike for other mob-related detachments during the entire 1930's and beyond. A prime example of such... none other than the outrageously sensationalized 1936 trial of Charles "Lucky" Luciano and eight other defendants. The charges were essentially based on the premise that Lucky and friends were operating nationwide prostitution rings, known as the "Combine" or "Combination." With the *murder for hire* division of Luciano's Mob Empire crumbling just a few years after that trial, well, utilizing a more marketable and distinguishing name was in the best interest of press, police, politicians and the DA's office. And so it was... *Murder Inc.* the moniker was born in early 1940.

And again, although selling newspapers was highly dependent on eye-popping, albeit often exaggerated headlines, when it came to this band of bloodthirsty brethren - the press was genuinely trying to reiterate the unconscionable extreme nature of this group. These gangsters were unlike anything the underworld had ever encountered before, and unlike anything the underworld has ever produced since. Their collective exploits were the stuff of contemporary horror films, replete with inhuman acts of the vilest kind. There eventually came to be fewer instances of quick and quiet gunshots to a target's head. To make the point very clear, many of the hits were carried out with frenzied bloodlust; enjoyment may even be an appropriate description. Weapons of a barbaric and terrifying nature were preferred over any typically expected gangland go-to choice. Death, essentially for these men, was an art and meant to invoke psychological terror into anyone and everyone.

Long before anyone outside the mob knew the intricacies of the "Combination," there were rumblings and outrages over the gangland wars in general– the injustice when known participants would arrogantly stroll out of virtually every police lineup. Unscathed, swaggering and above the law, such were some of these burgeoning young enforcers. An excellent example of the anger towards a lackadaisical legal system was made very clear in an op-ed piece penned nearly a decade before the world knew the true nature of the mob's killing machine.

In his September 1931 commentary, "The News To-Day," William Morris minced no words in his disgust for the manner in which gangsters were hauled in for atrocious crimes, and systematically released virtually every time. He used the example of six young men in particular.

"But there is another problem that cannot be treated as a form of social disease, but that must be faced by those who enforce our laws in order that citizens may live in peace. Here are six young men, the oldest twenty-seven years old, who already have 100 arrests chalked up against them, and who undoubtedly have sinned against the moral and legal codes many times one hundred times."

Though he could not have known at the time – Morris was so very precisely correct in forecasting further crimes of four named in the piece. Abe Reles, Harry Maione, Martin Goldstein and Harry Strauss would, a decade later, become the faces and poster boys of New York's most deadly hit squad.

Morris was not the first, nor was he the last, person to openly condemn the boldness of mobsters and an especially lax legal system. Judges, prosecutors, reporters and radio personalities began voicing outrage. A law was even established, basically, to make arresting gaggles of gangsters in fell swoops all the easier. Still, it seemed nothing could stop the frequency of bodies appearing in alleys, in dumps, in cars, in pits, in lakes and even on busy street corners. All the while, for almost an entire decade, nobody realized the underworld chaos they condemned was so vast, so complex and so intricately related.

And now back to mystery number one: Was it Harry Feeney who cleverly created the iconic phrase Murder Inc.?

The first arrests that led investigators to begin unravelling the complex organization had occurred in early February 1940. The use of *Murder Inc.* became commonplace in March. Feeney had covered the story early on and was often chatting it up with the King's County prosecutor's team. Some could argue Feeney was truly immersed from day one, so it would be reasonable to imagine him whipping up such an amazing descriptor – one that virtually every other news media source and investigative body of the law adopted as *the* term for this bizarre mob extension.

The Alternate Theory...

In July of 1975, syndicated entertainment writer Jack O'Brian addressed Murder Inc.'s origins in his column "On Broadway." He was harkening back to the good old days of the *World-Telegram* and how Harry Feeney was "The finest police reporter in N.Y. history." O'Brian also gave high praise to another of the *World-Telegram's* esteemed staff - rewrite man – Asa Bordages.

"Asa coined the 'Murder Inc.' title. Two days later someone told Asa to register it as a Hollywood film, but Murder Inc. had been snapped up about the moment Asa's story hit the newsstands."

O'Brian further explained in the column how registration of titles in Hollywood was based on the first claimant, and thus Bordages' creation was unavailable by the time he attempted the process. O'Brian also stated that Bordages did get his story told in film, but it was titled "Brooklyn U.S.A." and starred Humphrey Bogart. However, Bogart was never in a movie called "Brooklyn U.S.A." However, a film titled "The Enforcer" released in 1951 and featured Bogart as a crusading District Attorney. Going back before O'Brian's recollection, a column written in 1967 by another former *World-Telegram* reporter – Mel Heimer – stated Feeney "invented the name" and Asa Bordages wrote a *play* based on all the Murder Inc. characters, which had run on Broadway and was titled "Brooklyn U.S.A."

So then, whatever happened to the original phrase? The term "Murder Inc." became the title of a 1951 book by Burton Turkus and Sid Feder. Then in 1960, a film version based on that book, also titled "Murder Inc.," released with actor Peter Falk in the starring role. The phrase remained popular for use in everything from automobile ads to comic books to the name of a record label.

Iconic photographer Arthur "Weegee" Fellig, known for capturing stark and provocative images throughout New York City from 1935 to 1946, dubbed himself

"The Official Photographer of Murder Inc." His common nickname, *Weegee*, was spawned from an uncanny ability to arrive at newsworthy scenes often before police did – as though he used a Ouija Board. Many of his pictures, which he sold regularly to newspapers, depicted the arrests, deaths and aftermath of New York City's gangland wars.

૮ઠ ୧ଓ

Chapter 4

An Ensemble Cast

"You don't realize how big a thing this is."

– *Abe "Kid Twist "Reles, 1940*

From the kingpins to the street soldiers, prosecutors to the detectives, and hardened killers to not-so-innocent victims – the incredible list of characters from Murder Inc.'s decade of decadence could be envied by even the most creative character development in Hollywood. Truth is stranger than fiction; these people were very real, extraordinarily fascinating, and for some - their role in this crime drama perhaps blurred the lines between good and bad.

Who were these guys though, the ones chosen to carry out contracts on human life?

"It was an amazing, sick crew of homicidal maniacs," says former FBI agent Joaquin "Jack" Garcia.

Garcia, famously known by his mobster alter-ego *Jack Falcone* while infiltrating the Gambino family just a handful of years ago, also says trying to put Murder Inc. into a contemporary perspective is difficult because it truly was an anomaly.

"That's not going to happen today in the mob. We live in a different age. That gang of sociopaths -It would not be tolerated. They way law enforcement has evolved, it would be stopped or the mob would stop it."

Even during the murderous rampage years (1931-1940), the public was not laying down exactly, but upstanding law enforcement and political figures were at the mercy of limited crime solving resources. Garcia says the era of Murder Inc.'s existence was at a time when the mob literally "infiltrated every segment of society." That, paired with lacking science and technology to solve and/or connect crimes, made Murder Inc.'s way of life possible and profitable.

"There are 'shooters' in the mob today," Garcia explains, "but too many cameras, and now there's DNA, and too many 'cooperators'. Back then there was no CSI."

The crime "Syndicate" that evolved following the 1931 murders of Masseria and Maranzano was vast and gaining more ground by the day. Each of the bosses brought their own special rackets to the table, from industrial to gambling to unions to narcotics. Louis "Lepke" Buchalter had personally witnessed Abe Reles' crew strip lucrative rackets away from the notorious Shapiro Brothers, cut into Jack "Legs" Diamond's interests, and in time – probably predicted that same crew would remove the pesky Amberg Brother's from the criminal landscape as well. These observations seemed to avert a "human resource" nightmare. The best of the best cast were chosen, or so they thought.

Former FBI operative and author Ronald Fino, however, adds another concept as to who of the bosses settled on a more-confined and controlled group of killers.

"When the Syndicate was formed by Meyer Lansky, Louis Lepke, Lucky Luciano, Frank Costello et al.," says Fino, "it was Costello that wanted to control the numerous killings and limit them to Syndicate approval using the Brownsville and Ocean Hill group."

It's an interesting added theory, and very possible that Frank Costello had direct input on how to handle enforcement issues. Costello was always considered the diplomatic member of the Syndicate's directors. The title "Prime Minister of the Underworld" truly fit his style, approach and role within the annals of organized crime. Costello employed cash, gifts, favors, marketing tactics, and relationship-building – as opposed to violence – for gaining business. As unlikely as such a personality and technique would seem making decisions on the establishment of a murder team, a guy like Frank would certainly have been a voice of reason.

"The rationale behind this was to control the killings and send the right messages to those that acted on their own without approval etc," Fino adds. "It was working until the Mad Hatter used it to promote his own agenda."

Abe Reles, Harry Maione, Martin Goldstein, Harry Strauss, and Frank Abbandando – they all had worked in and knowledge of rackets, proved their mettle in gangland warfare and operated from a centralized area. Employing those men, and their handpicked associates, probably seemed more than logical to Lepke and/or the other reigning Syndicate bosses. A one-stop shop for the dirtiest of deeds, based in Brooklyn's Brownsville section; it was a near-perfect formula. The soldiers were respected and reliable, the pipeline of information was filtered through channels, the bosses were insulated, and if any of the hit squad did get pinched – a network of lawyers, bail money, favors and payoffs were in place.

Then, over the course of a few years, the killer Combination added more associates. Younger hoods such as "Julie" Catalano, "Cuppy" Migden, "Dukey" Maffetore and "Pretty" Levine were drawn into the allure of fancy cars, expensive clothes and street credibility displayed flamboyantly by the Brownsville Boys. More organizers and hands-on muscle was recruited from in and around Brooklyn. Among them, Louis Capone, Jack Parisi, Walter Sage, Emanuel "Mendy" Weiss, Charles "The Bug" Workman, Jacob

Drucker, Irving Cohen and the Bronx's Irving "Knadles" Nitzberg, were getting neck deep in the murder-for-hire.

Local properties were purchased, such as garages, for various Combination needs. A central headquarters was established, with additional friendly local bars, stores and restaurants to serve as satellite or emergency meeting spots. Rates and salaries were figured, as was a management structure and bonuses for "special" jobs. The system was designed to work seamlessly with the broader scope of the Syndicate's *national* reach. Mob affiliates in Detroit, Chicago, Cleveland and Los Angeles were able to request the services of the contract Combination's most willing and able workforce. But overall... the design of a murderous division was to keep the mob's *own* ranks in order, and again, limit violence.

The full extent of people, places and things involved in the Murder Inc. tale is virtually immeasurable, but here is a cheat-sheet of sorts, just to give a little organized breakdown on some of the names that popped up particularly during and after the actual discovery of Murder Inc. In no way is this list all-inclusive! Volumes could be written, would have to be written to include everything. We'll keep this the short and to-the-point version.

The Gangbusters	
John Harlan Amen	Special Prosecutor
Thomas E. Dewey	DA, NY County (Manhattan)
William O'Dwyer	DA, Kings County
Burton B. Turkus	Assistant DA, Kings County
Solomon Klein	Assistant DA, Kings County
William Deckelman	DA, Sullivan County
John Osnato	Detective
The Mob Bosses	
Charles "Lucky" Luciano	Louis "Lepke" Buchalter
Meyer Lansky	Jacob "Gurrah" Shapiro
Frank Costello	John "The Fox" Torrio
Benjamin "Bugsy" Siegel	Joe Adonis
Albert "The Mad Hatter" Anastasia (aka "Lord High Executioner")	
The Bad Guys	
Harry "Happy" Maione	Martin "Buggsy" Goldstein
Seymour "Blue Jaw" Magoon	Charles "The Bug" Workman
Max "The Jerk" Golob	Jacob "Jack" Drucker
Irving "Knadles" Nitzberg	Jack "Dandy" Parisi
Louis Capone	Emanuel "Mendy" Weiss
Frank "The Dasher" Abbandando	
Abe "Kid Twist" Reles (aka Albert Roth)	
Harry "Pittsburgh Phil" Strauss (aka Pep)	
Vito "Socks" Gurino (aka Chicken Head)	
Albert "Tick Tock" Tannenbaum (aka Allie)	
Irving "Big Gangi" Cohen (aka Jack Gordon)	

Associated Bad Guys	
Sholem "Sol" Bernstein	Abraham "Pretty" Levine
Oscar "The Poet" Friedman	Meyer "Mickey" Sycoff
Frank Carbo	Harry "Champ" Segal
Jacob "Cuppy" Migden	Carl "Mutt" Goldstein
Angelo "Julie" Catalano	Alexander Strauss
Louis "Duke" Maione	Sam "Dapper" Siegel
Louis "Tiny" Benson	Morris "Shep" Shapiro
Anthony "Duke" Maffetore (aka Dukey)	
Abraham, Israel and Lena Frosch	
The Ladies *(Some good, some bad, others somewhere in between)*	
Elsie "Tootsie" Feinstein	Helen Gourdine
Gertrude Gurino	Rose Gold
Florence Nestfield	Ruth Sewall
Anna Magoon	
Evelyn "Kiss of Death" Mittelman	
The Victims *A Mere Sampling*	
Joe "The Boss" Masseria	Salvatore Maranzano
Sam "Muddy" Kasoff	Hyman Yuran
Walter Sage	Irving "Puggy" Feinstein
Samuel "Tootsie" Feinstein	Irving Ashkenas
George "Whitey" Rudnick	James "Spider" Murtha
Norman Redwood	Alex "Red" Alpert
Morris Kessler	Morris Diamond
Peter Panto	Irving Penn

The Victims A Mere Sampling (continued)	
Joseph Rosen	Alvin Sydnor
Harry Millman	Charles "Chink" Sherman
Irving, Meyer and Willie Shapiro	
Harry "Big Greenie" Greenberg	
Arthur "Dutch Schultz" Flegenheimer	
Joseph and Louis "Pretty" Amberg	
Cesare Lattaro and Antonio Siciliano	

 G8 &0

Chapter 5

Strange Things Happen at Grandma's Place

'Midnight Rose' Gold

Dressed in matronly clothing, long white hair fixed in a neatly formed bun; the exterior appearance and demeanor was picture perfect. She fit the profile: a hardworking and humbly living immigrant trying to make her way to the American Dream. Rosie – as she was sometimes known – had a presence that literally personified the image of a grandmother. She truly seemed to be just an elderly darling. But then there's the dark and sinister truth behind it all.

The twice-married Rose Gold was a sixty-seven year old mother of four, grandmother of five, and the proprietor of a popular corner store in the Brownsville section of Brooklyn. Every day she would travel two miles from her home at 574 Vermont Street to work on the corner of Livonia and Saratoga – commonly known around town as "Midnight Rose's." The nondescript store addressed 779 was among many other establishments of retail and service lining the street. However, in the case of Rose's shop - the real estate adage, *"location, location, location,"* took on an entirely creepy and literal new meaning. Businesses certainly received good foot traffic in the area, but Rose's "all night" place was neatly tucked just near the above-running El tracks, and this particular position offered an added benefit of far more nefarious purpose, as fate would unveil one day.

For years, presumably, Rose Gold had been suspected of serving folks much more than cigars, sweets and soda. Still, it wasn't until the late 1930's that mere suspicion became full on investigations into what exactly was going on in that store. Rose's establishment wasn't a crime scene per se, but New York's equally enterprising investigators discovered the otherwise harmless grandma was involved with a bunch of "bad boys" and their very dynamic and extensive rackets.

Prohibition kept cops busy, but the post-prohibition era presented a new expanded beast to deal with. The first few years of the 1930's had become a time of major crackdown on New York's sprawling underworld network, replete with extortion, narcotics trafficking, shylock and prostitution rackets. The infamously mob-friendly political machine known as Tammany Hall had come under heavy scrutiny by legitimate political and law enforcement figures. Arthur "Dutch Schultz' Flegenheimer – known for his beer and numbers rackets in the Bronx and Harlem – had been under siege by the ambitious Thomas E. Dewey and his staff of prosecutors. Just after Dutch's untimely demise in 1935 (by fellow gang lords), Dewey metaphorically slayed the biggest dragon the mob has ever known – Charles "Lucky" Luciano in an outrageous and sensational 'prostitution' case. Luciano was served a 30 to 50 year sentence (1936). Next on the list of most wanted - garment district and drug network gangland gods – Louis "Lepke" Buchalter and Jacob "Gurrah" Shapiro. While business in the mob world was at its zenith moments during the 1930's, the decade also proved very dangerous times to be a gangster. If the law didn't get you, nervous friends and foes just might.

Within this time of mob smashing warfare, another zealot of gangbusters – Assistant Attorney General John Harlan Amen – began digging into strange relationships of Brooklyn's highly recognized but lower-tier bad boys, and how their various rackets were carried out. Seek and you will find, or so the saying goes. Amen had certainly sought out and uncovered some unusual connections, not the least of which had a link between a seemingly sweet old lady and a bunch of Jewish and Italian hoodlums with unbelievably long arrest records. The names Reles, Maione, Strauss *and* Goldstein kept popping up.

Rose Gold was extremely resourceful and savvy to the ways of Brooklyn's underworld inner workings, notwithstanding the fact she was functionally illiterate, able to scrawl little more than her own name. Despite her educational obstruct – Gold's store was a catalyst in some of the most brazen criminal exploits. Rose was a matriarch who coddled the young mobsters and enabled some of their most astounding criminal endeavors.

This was a family affair as well. Gold's son, her sister and sister-in-law, among those involved. And then there was the lovely Frosch family. Friends of Gold, Israel and Lena Frosch, with their son Abraham, ran the largest bail bonds racket in Brooklyn, always able to get the boys out of jail quickly. Sam "Dapper" Siegel, Gold's son from a previous marriage, had operated in numerous shady businesses, including lucrative loan shark and gambling rackets both in New York and Miami. His partner in crime – the 400-plus-pound Louis Benson, affectionately known as "Tiny." Much of their work was overseen by one Abraham "Kid Twist" Reles – a well-known Brooklyn gang leader.

Grandma's *boys* were the vilest, most recognized, feared and fearless men to perhaps ever roam the streets of New York continuously, together, for an entire decade. Abe Reles, Harry Maione, Martin Goldstein, Harry Strauss, Louis Capone, and a slew of other Brownsville and Ocean Hill toughs hung around the shop, inside the shop, and outside in the shadows of the EL train. Rose Gold didn't just provide for these boys, she profited. Sooner or later the law catches on to the flailing tentacles of any wide-stretching criminal reach. Once snagged, those tentacles are a pathway, leading investigators into the lair. So it was for Rose Gold's corner store.

So, what then truly put Rose Gold under the legal microscope? Initially, it was all about the bail. Gold came under scrutiny for the number of bail bonds pledged to her property. Thanks to her wonderful friends, the Frosch clan, the scheme was great for getting the boys out of detention is short order. However, once Amen completed his homework on this situation, Gold was snatched into custody. On May 4, 1939, she was accused of falsely swearing in posted bail bonds between the years 1934 to 1938; and officially charged with seventeen counts of first-degree perjury. John Harlan Amen wanted to make sure the old woman didn't skate out of jail on quick bail like so many of the hoodlums she helped had done.

Besides believing Gold was crucial to his case, Amen felt that others would likely want to silence her permanently if she was among the public again. He wasn't just referring to mobster threats; Gold was also related to two political figures. He pleaded to Supreme Court Justice McCurn for $75,000 bail in hopes it would keep her secure.

"She is the principal figure in at least three of the most vicious rackets in Brooklyn," Amen declared. "This candy store is the headquarters of a policy game, prostitution racket and similar enterprises, and it is easy to see why several persons would be interested in seeing that she is not available for trial."

Gold's attorney jumped up and immediately cried foul. The public defender was astounded by what he perceived as still a shockingly high bail, especially considering how frail his client was. He told the court Gold was a widow of twenty-five years, suffering from a heart ailment and certainly not a flight risk (because she would be in the care of her large and localized family). The plea for mercy seemed to work, at least for the moment. Court was recessed so a medical doctor could examine Mrs. Gold before the Justice would set bail.

Well then, who was this zealous public defender rushing to the aid of Rose Gold? We'll get to that surprise soon!

When court reconvened, McCurn listened as Amen questioned Dr. Lancellotti regarding any findings of "heart ailments or arteriosclerosis." The doctor said he found no obvious signs of any heart problems. Gold's counsel took to cross-examining, whereby the doctor and was forced to admit he couldn't conclusively determine all her health issues on such a quick examination, but still made it very clear that for her age she was in "fairly good" condition.

To seal up his request for a high bail, Amen fired off one more query, asking the doctor if the "shock" of going to jail would have any particularly harmful effect on Gold. Doctor Lancellotti replied, "From my examination, I can't say it would."

Justice McCurn set bail at $50,000 and Rose Gold was readied for a trip to the Women's Detention Center. As detectives escorted Gold through the courthouse hallway, her son Sam collapsed backwards, slid down the wall into a seated position, thus causing quite a stir. He was overcome with grief over his mother's indictment and incarceration, or so he wanted the camera-wielding reporters to capture on film. Yes indeed, Sam "Dapper" Siegel had put on quite a show, but it did not sway Lady Justice. Gold was taken to jail as planned. And Siegel? He went back to Brownsville and paced the street outside his mother's store, offering eager reporters only one comment regarding Rose – "Go ask the neighbors."

Less than a week had passed since Gold's incarceration when John Harlan Amen's office made more damning discoveries. Midnight Rose had over $150,000 in the bank – a helluva lot of dough for a tiny "stationary" store to be bringing in (later it was discovered to be over $400,000 across several accounts). Besides the large amount of cash on hand, employees of the Bank of Manhattan Company in Flatbush reported the illiterate Rose Gold often needed assistance filling out paperwork and that it was commonly believed she was actually doing banking for someone else, an unknown party. Some of the daily transactions Gold made were in amounts ranging from $5,000 to $10,000 at a time. Investigators concurred that there was absolutely no legitimate way her little store could be producing that amount of money.

While Gold was being thoroughly investigated, the Frosch family was indicted for their part in the bail scam. Although their attorney tried to have the charges dropped, Justice McCurn stood firm, maintaining the bond fraud was a very real and important part of the Governor's inquiry. Lena Frosch, who habitually frowned when not habitually dozing off during questioning, was deemed the chief "fixer" in almost every instance where the Reles gang members were arrested and needed bailed out. Frosch's role was not limited to merely posting the bail. She was accused of intimidating witnesses and paying off officials and/or jurors as well. The boys were well taken care of, thanks to the complex system headquartered out of an elderly grandmother's candy shop.

Things weren't looking very good for Rose and company, but a bizarre chain of events had been brewing secretly behind closed doors of Justice McCurn's office. Amen and one of his chief assistants met with McCurn only a month after Gold was levied the $50,000 bail – which she did not produce. Following the hearing, McCurn slashed the bail to $10,000. It came as a shock to the news media, which then reported the only details to emerge revealed Amen agreed to the amount and that Gold's attorney requested, after he produced an affidavit from Etta Ruberman (Gold's sister) listing all Mrs. Rose Gold's illnesses.

Shortly after the hearing, another of Gold's sisters, Fannie Ritow, posted the necessary bond collateral through the Continental Casualty Company. Rose Gold was released from the Women's Detention Center and went right back to running her store. Her boys were still very welcome to do business at 779 Saratoga as well.

But the story of this *Grandma* was far from over. The discoveries made and questions raised by Rose Gold's business practices and relationship to neighborhood gangsters began to crack the seal on a long running mystery. She would be visited again by investigators, some new and some old.

ഇ ൬

Chapter 6

Beginning of the End

"The board of directors talked it over and took a vote to decide whether the prospective victim should be stabbed, shot, strangled or bludgeoned to death. They then appointed an expert in the particular line selected."

– The Murder Inc. system as described by a spokesman for District Attorney William O'Dwyer, April 15, 1940

King's County District Attorney William O'Dwyer had only been in office a month, but was geared up to take on the mob just like his gang-busting colleagues, Thomas E. Dewey DA, of New York County and John Harlan Amen, special assistant to the U.S. Attorney General. O'Dwyer's brother, a police officer, had been killed by a stick-up man in the early 1930's, so Bill – who was a former police officer himself - took this mission personally. He was not alone in a desire to finally rid New York of racketeers; a solid staff of equally motivated assistants would enter history for rupturing the most unusual, frightening and destructive microcosm of underworld structure.

O'Dwyer had big shoes to fill though. It was 1940 and Dewey, a virtual celebrity by then, had prosecuted bootlegger and narcotics kingpin Irving "Waxey Gordon" Wexler, chased down the notorious "Beer Baron of the Bronx" Dutch Schultz, locked away the biggest prize Charles "Lucky" Luciano, and put out a nationwide manhunt for Louis "Lepke" Buchalter (who had recently turned himself in to federal agents). He wanted to get every well-known criminal behind bars. Now it can be argued as to whether or not Dewey was just driven by moral passion or more of a political motivation, but regardless of reasons – Dewey was a force to be reckoned with. Gangsters knew this. Dutch Schultz threatened to kill him, but even the mob bosses feared that would be even more detrimental, so the Dutchman was whacked by his own kind.

Harlan fought tooth and nail to break apart organized crime particularly in Brooklyn. It was his efforts that truly opened the can of worms on the murder Syndicate discoveries, though nobody knew it at the time. His investigation into the long-swirling suspicions regarding Rose Gold and her all-night candy store further cemented the belief that local gangsters had a loyal throng of enablers in a multitude of lucrative rackets.

Notwithstanding the overall cleanup effort in greater New York, neither everything nor everyone doing dirty deeds was rousted. The mess was convoluted and far reaching. However, O'Dwyer's office was destined to find and piece together the intricate and well-oiled Syndicate machinations – particularly its contract killing division. O'Dwyer's efforts, sort of, fit in between the methods of Amen and Dewey. Thomas Dewey's main focus was going directly after the big fish, hoping their removal from society would force a trickle-down effect. Amen was appointed to disinfect Brooklyn from bad elements – be them gangsters, or corrupt police and politicians.

Bill O'Dwyer appeared to be interested in catching lesser known fish. But, small never meant insignificant to the DA, and it had become very apparent to his staff and some determined detectives that hang-arounds and soldier types were likely going to provide overwhelming reams of testimony... all leading up to the top ranks. Again, they had no idea how far the organization stretched geographically or socially. The DA was, in many regards, in office at the right time and place. The stars somewhat aligned and it all began with a grieving mother's determination and a low level convict's personal vendetta.

The First Songbirds

Based on some curious information received in his office, O'Dwyer looked into an unsolved case from 1933. The story goes... Alex "Red" Alpert, still in his twenties, was shot to death because he wanted more of a share from the Combination rackets. Oh there were arrests for sure, but in usual fashion – nobody was held or convicted. His mother knew who was responsible; Red often expressed his fears aloud. She walked to police headquarters almost every day for years following his murder, expressing her intentions of never giving up on justice for her son. Finally, her prayers were answered.

Harry Rudolph, a small time crook, had been sitting in jail, stewing over some underworld issues he had knowledge of. One day Rudolph penned a note addressed to O'Dwyer's office stating he had information that would nail Alpert's killers. When the DA received and read the note, it moved him to immediately reopen the case and from there - the house of cards began to fall.

By the first week of February 1940, cops had picked up a total of the three men (two of whom Alpert's mother and Harry Rudolf professed were responsible for the Red Alpert slaying). Abe Reles and Martin Goldstein were known by cops thanks to their long rap sheet, subsequent releases, and therefore considered unlikely to talk. A swarthy, twenty-two year old, tight-lipped, low level hood named Anthony "Duke" Maffetore, now seemed more "breakable." Without much hard evidence for a murder charge, the trio was booked on vagrancy (a common go-to charge in such situations). The big timers were held in Brooklyn, but Dukey was placed in the Bronx, a jail known as "Singing School." Be it out of fear of long prison time, or worse yet – mob reprisal, Maffetore wasn't willing to utter a word. O'Dwyer and Detective John Osnato had begun to feel deep down that all those years of bodies being dumped in and around New York City could very well have something in common. Dukey was, eventually, going to open the floodgates – after a little reverse-psychology and clever police work was employed.

Dukey paced incessantly; worried a recording device was hidden. When he did speak, it generally was a question of why he should say anything at all. They pleaded with him to consider his boss's fancy clothing, jewels, salaries in comparison to his scraping by to feed his family, and how he would be the first thrown under the bus. "Dukey" Maffetore remained reticent. Okay then, thought O'Dwyer, now it's time to apply *Plan B*. Officers were ordered to strip the prisoner naked. With his once-steely nerves beginning to deteriorate, he stood exposed in the cold unwelcoming District Attorney's office.

"We have a tip," the DA casually informed Maffetore, "that you're going to be knocked off."

Maffetore stayed silent, although slight confusion paled his face. O'Dwyer looked the nude man up and down one more time, before adding – "We just want to be sure we can identify the corpse."

With that issuance of fear delivered, they told Dukey to dress and he was free to go. Concerned, but anxious to get away from the DA's office, Maffetore stepped outside to freedom. He had not made it very far down the street when a carload of gun-wielding men cut him off. "Come on Duke," one demanded. "You're going for a ride."

The wannabe tough guy fainted right there on the sidewalk. When he awoke – it was a mad dash back to the DA's office, screaming and crying for protection (is how O'Dwyer recalled it). The plan worked. A little mental trickery and four cops pretending to be thugs; Dukey was now theirs. Interrogators also knew that Maffetore had nothing to do with the Alpert murder. That's not what they wanted from him. What they did hope to get was nothing less than first-hand testimony against the hardcore killers and bosses. To further convince Dukey, Detective Osnato drew the "wife and family" card, offering a bleak future if gang lords had their way.

"I love my wife," Dukey declared. "I don't want to leave her. I'll talk."

Anthony "Duke" Maffetore unloaded information connecting Abe "Kid Twist" Reles as the direct man in charge of a murder-for-profit racket. And for further verification, Dukey told the investigators his pal, Abraham "Pretty" Levine, could corroborate everything. That's just what they did – grabbed Levine and quickly hid both men in a hotel room for their own safety. This was a very dangerous situation, so precautions were not taken lightly. The men Maffetore and Levine named were clearly understood to be merciless killers of, most especially, stoolpigeons.

Both men were essentially on-call car thieves and chauffeurs for the group known as "The Combination," yet even in low level positions were often present or privy to some very gruesome crimes. This fact placed them in great danger with the mob and the cops.

Levine, understandably, also tried to remain silent, at first. Police allowed Maffetore to have a lengthy talk with his buddy, which worked in convincing Levine to come clean as well. He also had a young family to worry about, which trumped mob loyalty.

Both men kept mentioning an old familiar name around Brooklyn – Abe Reles. "Kid Twist" they called him. Cops, judges, prosecutors and rival mobsters all knew who Kid Twist was. The young hoods also sang about the Brooklyn candy store owned by Rose Gold, and of the resort areas in and around Monticello and Loch Sheldrake in Sullivan County. Specifically mentioning how bodies were often dumped there. Levine even admitted that, under the direction of Martin "Buggsy" Goldstein, he personally stabbed to death a man he only knew as "Jack" – later sinking that victim into the depths of Sheldrake. And, they talked about Albert Tannenbaum family having owned a resort in Sullivan County, plus Jack Drucker's old man's farm.

The information would have been totally mindboggling if it weren't for the massive case files of unsolved murders dating back nine years that prosecutors were acquainting themselves with. O'Dwyer had learned of at least three dozen murders that could then, possibly, be attributed or connected to the select group of killers Maffetore and Levine were naming. The otherwise convoluted mess of gang war history was finally beginning to make sense.

Sweeps week was underway. Police were sent out in full force, grabbing up everyone whose name had been uttered by the duo. Among the first wave were Harry "Pittsburgh Phil" Strauss, Harry "Happy" Maione, and Frank "The Dasher" Abbandando. O'Dwyer's onslaught also captured Albert "Tick Tock" Tannenbaum, Seymour "Blue Jaw" Magoon, Angelo "Julie" Catalano, Meyer "Mickey" Sycoff, and Oscar "The Poet" Friedman. Family members of known Combination gangsters were not spared from the massive round up either. Anyone even remotely thought to be connected to the group was hauled in for questioning. Some of the top perpetrators went into hiding, a few offered to turn state witness right off the bat, and others scowled at the authorities with an expectation of yet again walking right back out the prison gates.

And then O'Dwyer received yet another letter – this one penned by Abe "Kid Twist" Reles and delivered by his wife Rose (her name was also listed as *Jennie* in some newspapers). Reles had been sitting in a cell pondering the rumors some of his boys had been picked up. Worse yet, that those associates were squealing. The image of Sing Sing Prison's electric chair surely became seared into Kid Twist's brain. To top it all off, Mrs. Reles shared some important news - Abe was going to be a father again. Under such duress even the most hardcore tough guys tend to cave. Reles wanted O'Dwyer to hear his story in hopes of leniency once the Combination secrets were fully exposed. Reles was perhaps the most violent and hardhearted member of the murderous entourage, and therefore making the first move was his top priority to save his own skin.

The prosecutor told Kid Twist he would do everything in his power to help, but explained there were no guarantees – "If you come clean and stand up during trial, I'll take it into consideration. Beyond that I'll promise you nothing."

Abe Reles was everything and much more than O'Dwyer could've asked for. The Brownsville bad guy, once a stand-up gangster with a resume of crimes a mile high (yet never any lengthy jail time), had become a desperate and weakened shell of that past bravado. He told O'Dwyer of murders he personally committed, murders he plotted, murders committed by others and most importantly – who some of the men were actually calling in those "orders." And best of all – he was willing to tell it all to a grand jury.

Albert "Tick Tock" Tannenbaum's parents owned a resort near Loch Sheldrake, where many patrons came for bootleg liquor and gambling. Albert met Jacob "Gurrah" Shapiro and Harry "Big Greenie" Greenberg in 1925. He was offered a job at $35 a week by the gangsters, which eventually ushered him into the murder-for-hire division.

Meier (Meyer) "Mickey" Sycoff is perhaps one of the least known members of the Reles gang/Murder Inc. stool pigeons. Although not the most crucial witness within the DA's protection, his history, specifically in 1935, directly connected him as being in usury/shylock business dealings with the Reles gang members, including Carl "Mutt" Goldstein and George "Whitey" Rudnick. Another lesser discussed witness, Oscar Friedman, was responsible for disposing of

Murder Inc.'s stolen cars. He pointed investigators to several junkyards where the parts could be found. Friedman, called "The Poet" for allegedly always reading from a poetry book, later told reporters the book of sonnets had been planted on him. "I can barely even write," he later told reporters. "But I can play poker!"

CR RO

THE MURDER INC.

Photos

1930
*Victims of the Castellammarese War Steven Ferrigno
and Alfred Mineo Ambushed outside 706 Pelham Bay
Parkway following a meeting with Joe "The Boss"
Masseria, to whom they were loyal. The assassins
were reputedly from Salvatore Maranzano's faction -
bitter enemies of Masseria.*
(C. Cipollini Collection)

1930
Meyer and Irving Shapiro Not dead (yet) - just bored
to sleep after lengthy questioning in gangland murder
investigation. The Shapiro boys ran rackets in
Brooklyn, until Abe Reles decided it was time for the
Shapiros to go. Following some battles back and forth,
the Shapiro boys eventually knocked off, one by one.
First to be killed was Irving in 1931. His brother Meyer
followed that same year. The removal of the Shapiros
was impressive to Louis "Lepke" Buchalter, which
certainly helped secure Abe Reles' gang a spot on the
new Syndicate team. A third brother, Willie Shapiro,
was allegedly burried alive in 1934 by the then-fully-
formed "Combination," aka Murder Inc.
(C. Cipollini Collection)

1935
Martin "Buggsy" Goldstein Buggsy and Harry
"Pittsburgh Phil" Strauss surrendered to police after the
murder of Morris Kessler and Joseph Amberg. "The
papers list me as Public Enemy No. 6," Buggsy
arrogantly complained. "That's a lousy rating. I've
worked hard. And I hope to get a better rating than
that."
(C. Cipollini Collection)

1935
Morris Kessler and Joseph Amberg Kessler, a chauffer
to the Amberg brothers, lies in the foreground;
Amberg in the background. Both were found shot to
death in a Brooklyn garage at 385 Blake Avenue.
There were allegedly three assailants, with pistols and
shotguns, dressed in mechanics outfits, accompanied
by a fourth man wearing a business suit. Initially,
police suspected Goldstein, Strauss and Louis Capone
were involved. Further investigations suggested Harry
Maione was present as well.
(C. Cipollini Collection)

1935
A bloody scene at the Palace Chop House.
October 23, Arthur "Dutch Schultz" Flegenheimer and
his men were gunned down during dinner at the
Newark, NJ restaurant located at 12 East Park Street.
(C. Cipollini Collection)

1937
Martin "Buggsy" Goldstein and Seymour "Blue Jaw"
Magoon questioned for their involvement in a painters'
union racket.
(C. Cipollini Collection)

1940
Anthony "Duke" Maffetore, Abraham "Pretty" Levine
and DA William Deckelman
(C. Jones Collection)

1940
Oscar "The Poet" Friedman. The Combination go-to guy for disposing of stolen vehicles. Oscar was a fraud though. He duped his clients into thinking he had a magical method for making vehicles vanish. In reality, he simply dumped car parts in junk yards and collected his fee from the unknowing gangsters. (C. Cipollini Collection)

1940
Murder Inc.'s Junkyard
Michael Votta's junkyard in Brooklyn was searched by
police. Oscar "The Poet" Friedman pointed
investigators to several such yards where the remains
of stolen vehicles and "murder" cars could be found.
Volta was held as a material witness in the Murder
Inc. investigation.
(C. Cipollini Collection)

Abraham "Kid Twist"
Reles

Harry "Pittsburgh Phil"
Strauss

Martin "Buggsy"
Goldstein

Harry "Happy" Maione

1938
Angelo "Julie" Catalano
(Burton B. Turkus Papers, Special Collections, Lloyd
Sealy Library, John Jay
College of Criminal Justice)

1931
Jack "Cuppy" Migden
(Burton B. Turkus Papers, Special Collections,
Lloyd Sealy Librar,
John Jay College of Crimminal Justice)

1940
Harry "Pittsburgh Phil" Strauss, Harry "Happy Maione,
Frank "The Dasher" Abbandando
(C. Cipollini Collection)

1940
The body of Hyman Yuran is exhumed from a lime pit
near Loch Sheldrake NY. Yuran was marked for death
by Louis "Lepke" Buchalter and the murder was
carried out by members of Murder Inc. Investigators
were led to the burial site by Sholem "Sol" Bernstein -
a regular getaway driver for the killing crew. Yuran
was kidnapped from his Brooklyn home, killed and
buried in 1938, but Coroner Dr. Lee R. Thompkins was
able to identify the badly decomposed body by dental
records.
(C. Cipollini Collection)

1940
William O'Dwyer
District Attorney
Spearheaded the assault on
Brooklyn's murder for hire
Syndicate.
(C. Cipollini Collection)

1940
Burton Turkus, Martin "Buggsy" Goldstein,
Harry "Pittsburgh Phil" Strauss
Indicted for the murder of Irving "Puggy" Feinstein
Buggsy and Phil plead not guilty.
(C. Cipollini Collection)

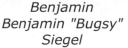
Benjamin "Bugsy" Siegel

Isadore "Izzy" Burnstein

"Siegel will try to restore order. He will be a field director, and with Bernstein — mark out those who must go," - statement made by District Attorney William O'Dwyer in April 1940.

1940
Investigators in New York were alarmed upon information suggesting two of gangdom's most feared entities had arrived to presumably "clean house" of any and all squealers.

Bugsy was an original boss of the Syndicate and Izzy was a boss from Detroit's Purple Gang.
(C. Cipollini Collection)

1940
Harry "Happy" Maione and
Harry "Pittsburgh Phil" Strauss
Indicted for the murder of George "Whitey" Rudnick.
Prosecutors quickly severed Strauss from this case
and added Frank Abbandando.
(C. Cipollini Collection)

1940
John Torrio, Ciro Terranova, Little Augie Pisano,
Joe Adonis Prosecutors announced in early April
that Reles named these four as "Directors" of
Murder Inc. That list changed dramatically grew as
investigations continued.
(C. Cipollini Collection)

1940
Burton Turkus and Solomon Klein
Assistant District Attorneys prepare for the first of
Murder Inc. trials on May 8th.
(C. Cipollini Collection)

1935
Helen Gourdine. Harry, "Happy" Maione's love interest. She often shared stories with her family of being the only person of color permitted inside the infamous "Midnight Rose's" and having met the man she knew was called the "Judge"- Louis "Lepke" Buchalter.
(Courtesy of Michael Gourdine)

1939
Mrs. Rose Gold (left) and others tend to her son Sam
"Dapper" Siegel upon his fainting spell after hearing
his mother was being indicted. Gold was the proprietor
of Midnight Rose's all night candy shop in Brooklyn.
Known for racketeering activity within the shop, the
discovery of Murder Inc.'s activities would surface a
year later.
(C. Cipollini Collection)

1939
Midnight Rose's
Candy, Cigars, Stationary Store
(C. Cipollini Collection)

1934. Beer Garden at #699 Ralph Avenue, Brooklyn.
Blood on floor, over turned chairs, the aftermath of a
bar-fight and robbery that left Vito Gurino with a
fractured skull. No witness could positively identify
who or what actually transpired, which in turn secured
the dismissal of both Gurino and Harry "Happy"
Maione from charges.
(C. Cipollini Collection)

1940
Elsie Feinstein aka Mrs. Tootsie Feinstein with Attorney Joseph Wohl. Elsie was held on charges of perjury. Though claiming to not know any of her husband's killers, Albert "Tick Tock" Tannenbaum gave prosecutors a 16mm home video showing Elsie on a beach in Miami with members of Murder Inc., including Tannenbaum (who owned the camera) and Charles "The Bug" Workman.
(C. Cipollini Collection)

1940
Evelyn Mittelman
aka "Kiss of Death" girl.
Girlfriend of Murder Inc. henchman
Harry "Pittsburgh Phil" Strauss
(C. Cipollini Collection)

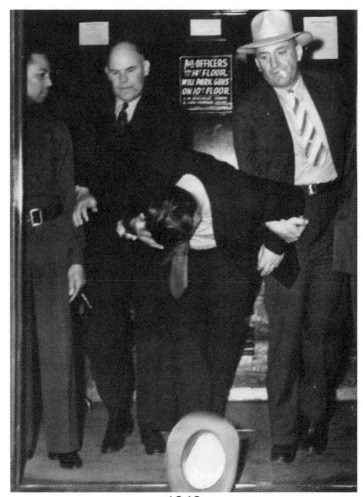

1940
Irving Cohen also Jack Gordon
Bit part actor is apprehended in Los Angeles
for the murder of Walter Sage
(C. Cipollini Collection).

*1938
Frank "Big Boy" Davino
Convicted for murder of
fireman Thomas J. Hitter.
Davino was not really a
member of Murder Inc., but
because he was frequently
shuttled to and from appeals
court with Maione &
Abbandando - he was guilty
by association in the local
press coverage.*

*1940
Harry "Happy" Maione & Frank "The Dasher"
Abbandando They listened to the grim death sentence
issued by Judge Franklin Taylor.
(C. Cipollini Collection)*

1941
Charles "The Bug" Workman
Pleaded no defense in charges he murdered Dutch
Schultz in 1935
(C Jones Collection)

1931
Harry Greenberg
The longtime pal of
Lepke, Gurrah & Bugsy
Siegel -
he became the mentor or
catalyst that brought
Albert
"Tick Tock" Tannenbaum
into the Syndicate.
(C. Cipollini Collection)

1939
Harry "Big Greenie" Greenberg
aka George Schechter
Hiding under an assumed name in Los Angeles,
Greenberg was killed by Frankie Carbo (the shooter),
Albert Tannenbaum (the distractor) and Benjamin
"Bugsy" Siegel (the getaway driver).
(C. Cipollini Collection)

1940
Harry "Champ" Segal and Frank Carbo Both men were implicated in the murder of Harry Greenberg.
(C. Cipollini Collection)

1940
Albert Tannenbaum and Abe "Kid Twist" Reles The pair testified in Los Angeles implicating Benjamin "Bugsy" Siegel in the murder of Harry "Big Greenie" Greenberg, aka George Schacter.
(C. Cipollini Collection)

1939
Louis "Lepke" Buchalter
Surrendered to J. Edgar Hoover to face narcotics
charges, expecting to be protected from New York
authorities who wanted him for the murder of Joseph
Rosen. The scenario played out much differently, as
Lepke was eventually turned over to New York. He
was the only mob boss to ever be executed.
(C. Jones Collection)

1936
Joseph Rosen
Murdered in his candy store.
Lepke pushed Rosen out of the trucking business, but later gave him a candy store to run. Rosen still wasn't happy and made threats. The killers were thought to be Mendy Weiss and Pittsburgh Phil, with Louis Capone directing the plot.
(Burton B. Turkus Papers, Special Collections, Lloyd Sealy Library, John Jay College of Criminal Justice)

1940
Martin "Buggsy" Goldstein and Harry "Pittsburgh Phil"
Strauss on train to Sing Sing Prison. Sentenced to
death for murder of Irving "Puggy" Feinstein.
(C. Cipollini Collection)

1941
Louis Capone and Emanuel "Mendy" Weiss on train to
Sing Sing Prison. Sentenced to death for murder
of Joseph Rosen.
(C. Cipollini Collection)

1940
Harry "Pittsburgh Phil" Strauss and
Martin "Buggsy" Goldstein
escorted by Sheriff James W. Mangano
through the gates of Sing Sing Prison.
(C. Cipollini Collection)

Old Sparky
Sing Sing Prison's most menacing occupant - the
electric chair.
Among Murder Inc.'s most notorious to meet their
maker on this device:
Harry "Pittsburgh Phil" Strauss,
Martin "Buggsy" Goldstein,
Harry "Happy" Maione,
Frank "The Dasher" Abbandando,
Louis Capone, Emanuel "Mendy" Weiss, and
Louis "Lepke" Buchalter
(Courtesy of Arthur Nash, New York City
Gangland Collection)

1950
Jack "The Dandy" Parisi
Dandy sneers at photographer while a detective looks on. Parisi was one of the Murder Inc. boys who managed to "walk" in every case he was connected to. The 1939 Bronx murder of music publisher Irving Penn, however, was a case of mistaken identity. Cuppy Migden pointed out Penn as the target, Parisi shot him, Seymour Magoon sped them away in the getaway car. It was soon realized they had killed the wrong man. The intended target was a Philip Orlovsky, a garment industry union boss - who not only lived in the same building as Penn, but also looked very similar in physical stature.
(C. Cipollini Collection)

1951
Albert "Lord High Executioner" Anastasia
Wearing dark glasses, the Murder Inc. boss tried to
avoid the Kefauver Hearings with a medical condition -
conjunctivitis. Though he managed
to avoid the major Murder Inc. trials over the years,
the Kefauver committee did not excuse him and he
was forced to appear for questioning.
(C. Cipollini Collection)

Persons of Interest:
Between 1957 and 1958, the investigation into Albert
Anastasia's murder continued. Included among the
throng of individuals brought in for questioning;
George Uffner, Frank Erickson and Meyer Lansky.
Erickson and Uffner were nabbed together in
December of 1957. Erickson remained very tight-
lipped and Uffner denied knowing Anastasia, except to
say, "Only heard of the slain gangster. Lansky was
picked up in 1958 while on a "visit" to New York. He
too was released shortly after a battery of
questions.

Meyer Lansky
(C. Cipollini Collection)

George Uffner
(Uffner Family Source

Frank Erickson
(C. Cipollini Collection)

1946
Auto Dealer Ad
The phrase Murder Inc. found its way into every segment of society after the highly publicized prosecutions commenced
(C. Cipollini Collection)

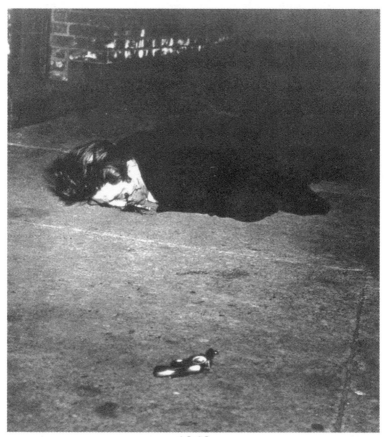

1940
"Slain Gangster, Hell's Kitchen"
Photographed by the iconic Arthur "Weegee" Fellig
(C. Cipollini Collection)

෪ ෨

Chapter 7

All Hell Breaks Loose

"You don't know what a favor you're doing me. I was never so glad to see a cop in my life! They were going to rub me out."

– Angelo "Julie" Catalano, 1940

What?! The guiltiest of all, Abraham "Kid Twist" Reles, was talking to prosecutors? That must've been the ultimate delirium-causing query for any member of the murder Combination. Worse yet, Reles was just one of *many* who sought refuge in the welcoming arms of District Attorney William O'Dwyer. Word travels fast in Brooklyn, but even faster up the ranks to those who were ultimately in charge. Reles' cooperation had already provided a laundry list of associated parties, and William O'Dwyer wanted even more people taken into custody. Some of those already rounded up were kept for their own safety because of one very real concern: When rumblings of "rats" reach the desks of Syndicate leaders – even more contracts are channeled back to the remaining Combination trigger men.

From his holding cell in Tombs Jail, Harry "Happy" Maione issued a warning through the underworld grapevine, specifically addressing DA William O'Dwyer's ambitious rundown.

"That fellow in Brooklyn wants to get busy. Well, we'll keep him busy. We'll drop packages all over Brooklyn for him to pick up."

The district attorney's office did not take the threat lightly, knowing "packages" meant corpses. His office had learned from Reles, and a few other members-turned-witnesses, the identities of victims, how some contracts were for a fee of only a few bucks, others in the hundreds, and the lieutenants earned a weekly salary along with valuable shares of certain rackets. It was time to move quickly, so prosecutors across the area sought to finalize who would be used as witnesses, who were material witnesses and of course – which was going to be tried for which murders.

Throughout the process, many individuals had to be placed under constant supervision. O'Dwyer had already and quite inadvertently saved the lives of Anthony "Duke" Maffetore, Abe "Pretty" Levine, and "Julie" Catalano simply by arresting them. It was learned later that Martin "Buggsy" Goldstein and Harry "Pittsburgh Phil" Strauss had actually set a date for some of the young hangers-on to be eliminated.

Spring was in the air, denizens were still being rousted, witnesses being queried and cases were drawn up for the first prosecutions. The DA's fears of mob revenge were exacerbated as every week passed from March to April. More revelations were presented to his office the deepened the murky waters of the what was now officially being called *Murder Inc.* A few of the alleged killers had gone on the lamb since the first roundup took place. This was a dangerous scenario for two reasons: fugitives may try to silence potential talkers, or fugitives could fall victim to silencers.

Conspiracy, in tandem with renegades, was another issue plaguing the prosecutor's efforts. Upon Maione's prison cell issued orders, Vito "Socks" Gurino, or "The Torpedo" as Happy referred to him, had paid at least two unquestioned visits to the jail where another witness – Joe "The Baker" Liberto – was being held. Gurino was on a mission to sway or warn Liberto and others to not cooperate with authorities. This infuriated O'Dwyer's staff because Gurino himself was a fugitive with several murder indictments.

The fear instilled by Happy Maione's threat was compounded by news that two out-of-towners had come to New York for a little cleanup work in early April. It was revealed that Benjamin "Bugsy" Siegel and Isadore "Izzy" Bernstein had been staying at the Ambassador Hotel in Manhattan. Siegel, a founding member and top boss in the Syndicate, had traveled from Southern California and Izzy Bernstein was a member of the infamously deadly Purple Gang in Detroit. Their reputations alone delivered implicit dread.

Scott M. Burnstein, author of *The Detroit True Crime Chronicles: Tales of Murder and Mayhem in the Motor City*, is also a relative of the infamous Purple Gang's Bernstein brothers. Addressing an issue common during reporting of gangland's heyday era – the habitual error of names – Burnstein sets the record straight on Izzy. "The press was misspelling their name; it was Burnstein, not Bernstein."

As to why any Purple member would have entered the theatre of Murder Inc.'s downfall era, Burnstein explains power and very close ties between Detroit and New York kingpins had a lot to do with it.

"Abe Burnstein (Izzy's brother) was probably the most powerful Jewish wise guy in America in the early 20th century other than Meyer Lansky. Abe and Meyer were close friends and business partners in oil deals in Mississippi and Louisiana after Prohibition."

Indeed the Purples and New York's Syndicate were closely allied, personally and professionally. William O'Dwyer clearly understood that any visit from a top Syndicate guy with a top Purple would mean nothing less than bloodshed.

"Siegel will try to restore order," O'Dwyer said in a statement to press. "He will be a field director, and with Bernstein – mark out those who must go."

The DA also learned that Murder Inc. was likely responsible for the 1937 shooting death of Harry Millman in a crowded Detroit deli. Thanks to the wealth of information provided by his bevy of talkative bad boys, the DA's staff was able to attribute, with a fair amount of confidence, that Millman's death was carried out by at least two of Murder Inc.'s most notable lieutenants.

But before O'Dwyer's team of investigators and detectives could act on the information relating to Bugsy and Izzy, word of such imminent arrests reached the duo. Both had quickly left the city before O'Dwyer's force could bring them in. It wasn't a total loss for prosecutors; they certainly felt some relief in knowing the notorious pair fled *before* carrying out any gangland purge.

More Sensational Namedropping:

For the 1935 murder of gang boss Arthur "Dutch Schultz" Flegenheimer, it was widely understood or assumed that Charles "Lucky" Luciano and John "The Fox" Torrio had issued the contract. They were "untouchable" of course, because that's how the murder Combination was designed – to insulate bosses. Schultz's murder was eventually pinned on Charles "The Bug" Workman. However, after William O'Dwyer's fact finding frenzy began putting pieces together – Lucky Luciano was brought up again. O'Dwyer implicated Luciano not only as a Syndicate boss with the power to employ Murder Inc.'s services, but that the incarcerated kingpin directly ordered the contract murder of a low level drug dealer named Sam "Muddy" Kasoff in 1934.

Possibly, because Luciano was already serving time for a 1936 compulsory prostitution conviction, there was no real effort to delve any further into the accusation. The DA's hands were certainly full with all the people, places and things on the front burner. O'Dwyer did however want to pursue another jailed Syndicate boss – Louis "Lepke" Buchalter. The DA believed Lepke also called upon the murder division's services, but at the time – had no idea he was the literal 'boss' of Murder Inc.

Other Syndicate honchos were mentioned as well. Abner "Longy" Zwillman, who was a member of the shadowy Seven Group in the bootlegging era, was a person of interest. Joe Adonis was implicated by Reles as having called in orders, as was another soon-to-be highly controversial figure – Albert Anastasia.

Then, it was the moment to start actually putting some of indicted men on trial. "Happy" Maione and Frank "The Dasher" were first on the list. William O'Dwyer's staff was ready for war.

Midnight Rose Revisited:

There was no shortage of unbelievable twists and surprises within the seedy tales and revelations as the DA sifted through a dark past. Old names were new again. The most fascinating irony involved Midnight Rose and her former counsel. The fiery public defender, who only a year prior rallied for the release of the poor sickly shopkeeper, had since become Assistant District Attorney, working under William O'Dwyer. Burton B. Turkus' job was to swiftly prosecute as many members of the killing machine dubbed "Murder Inc." as humanly possible. Gold and

Turkus were destined to meet again, but this time as adversaries.

In May of 1940, prosecutors put Anthony "Duke" Maffetore on the stand to testify against the first pair of Murder Inc. henchman brought to trial – Harry "Happy" Maione and Frank "The Dasher" Abbandando. Dukey's testimony confirmed what John Harlan Amen's investigation (which included wiretaps on Midnight Rose's phone) had theorized – the Reles gang used the place for much more than a hangout. Rose Gold's nondescript little shop served as the headquarters for the most brutal and widespread hit squad in gangland history.

Turkus: What I want to know is, was Saratoga and Livonia Avenues, that corner, one of the corners you used to hang around?

Maffetore: Yes sir.

Turkus: What is on that corner?

Maffetore: Candy store.

Turkus: Whose candy store was there in May 1937, do you know?

Maffetore: Dapper's candy store.

Turkus: Dapper who?

Maffetore: Siegel.

Turkus: Was that an all-night candy store?

Maffetore: What do you mean, if it was open all night?

Turkus: That is right.

Maffetore: It was open all night.

Turkus: Twenty-four hours a day?

Maffetore: Yes, sir.

Turkus: Who else ran the candy store besides Dapper Siegel?

Maffetore: His mother.

Rose Gold, aka *Midnight Rose* and *Brownsville Rose*, had never been an easy nut to crack. Nevertheless, the cards were still stacked against her for the perjury indictment dating back to John Harlan Amen's efforts in 1939. Turkus grilled his former client on her establishment's "other" uses.

"Why do you allow hoodlums to hang out in your store?" asked Turkus.

"Why don't the police keep them out," Gold fired back. "Can I help it who comes in my store?"

Another of the prosecution team then queried, "Do you know Pittsburgh Phil?"

Gold again offered a sharp tongued reply, "Pittsburgh, Chicago, San Francisco... what do I know about them? I was never out of Brooklyn in my life."

Then *something* happened, just before Gold was due in court on June 3, 1940 which persuaded her to plead guilty to seven of the counts she faced. Was it that two of her store's hangarounds – Maione and Abbandando – were facing impending doom? Or, some other gloomy scenario she foresaw? Supreme Court Justice McCrate accepted the plea, but did not sentence her immediately. In fact, McCrate had been quite lenient on two other women involved in the bail bond perjury, suspending both their sentences. Regardless of why she took a plea, it looked like Rose made a wise decision. She was able to quietly fadeout of the Murder Inc. pandemonium.

Other Interesting Characters:

District Attorney William O'Dwyer's swift roundup of virtually everyone and anyone associated with the murder Syndicate was replete with an amazing cross-section of individuals. Although many of them were dismissed almost as fast as they were hauled in, some were found to have reputations and backgrounds that almost rivaled those of the top gangland killers in custody.

Evelyn Mittelman

Following the arrest and indictments against Harry "Pittsburgh Phil" Strauss, a young woman would accompany Straus's brother Alex on jailhouse visits. She listed her relationship as "sister," but something unusual piqued the curiosity of prosecutors. She did not resemble either of the Strauss brothers in the slightest, and suddenly went from a blond to a brunette. Perhaps nothing that unusual to the casual observer, but it was enough for Burton Turkus to start inquiring about this sister. Turns out, she was Pittsburgh Phil's girlfriend for the past five years, and there was more! Evelyn Mittelman had sobriquet of her own, based on a sordid past that Turkus quickly discovered. She was called the "Kiss of Death Girl" – at least three of her previous lovers (some news reports claimed it was five) died while dating her. Each beau was, so it is said, knocked off by each subsequent suitor. Evelyn had a way of inspiring her *new* man to whack the current boyfriend. The last hapless Romeo fell victim to Pittsburgh Phil and company, having been weighted down in a Sullivan County lake.

This was very enlightening for the prosecution staff indeed. Mittelman was taken into custody as a material witness. Turkus quickly came to believe she knew the inner workings of Murder Inc. and requested she be held on $50,000 bail, stating in the application that she "knows all there is to know about how this Syndicate worked."

Louis Maione

Happy Maione's younger brother often explained his occupation was that of a "shoemaker" and later as a florist. He did in fact own several flower shops by 1940, but his résumé suggested a frequent dip in the underworld, especially during the early 1930's. Back then it was not uncommon for Harry and Louis, or "Duke" as he was known, to be arrested together. One of the more unusual cases involved a robbery charge in 1932. In late July, the pair gained entrance to an apartment at 1030 Park Place by telling the occupant, Edward Valentine, they were "inspectors." The tenant let them in and both Maiones proceeded to beat Valentine with the butts of revolvers before binding and gagging him. The duo took over $400 but before leaving – beat the victim into unconsciousness because he didn't know about a "safe" the robbers were seeking. The assaulted man identified the Maiones in a police station lineup that August, but the case went through a series of mistrials. And then in April 1933 – on the fourth attempt to try the Maiones, an even more bizarre event led to Louis and Harry's dismissal. Valentine had been committed to Brooklyn State Hospital earlier in the month. Psychiatrists told the court Valentine was insane, suffering specifically from Paresis – a form of neurosyphilis.

Louis, like his infamous brother, was obviously a familiar face in law enforcements' rolodex of resident gangsters, so O'Dwyer's staff being interested in speaking with him was natural. A manhunt was issued for "Duke" but he was already in jail on a vagrancy charge, to which his attorney argued was nonsense by telling the court that a vagrant is not someone who owned three Brooklyn floral shops. In early April 1940, Assistant DA J. William Keogh of O'Dwyer's staff opposed the writ for Maione's release saying, "A perfect front for a person who's not connected with flower shops."

O'Dwyer wanted Louis kept in custody for two reasons: He was a witness to the 1935 murder of John "Spider" Murtha and information suggested brother

Happy wanted him to carry out hits on other witnesses. Trying to hold "Duke" was futile though. He eventually gained release – which caused uproar again in 1942. Harsh criticism was issued by William O'Dwyer against Judge George W. Martin. The then-retired judge had issued Maione $400 dollars in compensation, essentially reparation, for having been held as a material witness during the trial of Max "The Jerk" Golob. O'Dwyer protested to the Appellate Division, arguing Maione was not an innocent witness, but was directly involved with the killers of "Spider" Murtha in 1935. O'Dwyer's appeal was tossed out.

Frank "Little Frankie" Gallucio

Now here was an underworld character with a legendary reputation. Gallucio didn't exactly resemble the stereotypical tough guy, but one specific altercation in the 1920's put him the mob's history books. Gallucio was the man, or so the story goes, that put the infamous scar on Al Capone's cheek. Instead of earning him a death sentence, the slashing incident gained the respect of the very man he mutilated. Capone reputedly hired "Little Frankie" as a bodyguard.

In late March 1940, O'Dwyer had Gallucio brought in as a person of interest. He was questioned for a few hours and then released. Ironically, after his incident with Capone, the knife-savvy Gallucio went on to become a barber. That career choice garnered some ridicule from police when he was picked up on a vagrancy charge in 1941. "Do you still use a knife, Frankie?" A detective asked, hoping to draw Gallucio into a pending joke. "No," he replied. "A razor. I'm a barber."

Elsie Feinstein

Sam "Tootsie" Feinstein was ready to take a legitimate path in life. He began saying as much, which was not a good idea for a guy involved in the mob. On May 10, 1939 – Sam was taken for a ride by some of his pals, "The Bug" Workman among them. He of course never returned, but his wife Elsie was given an envelope, weekly, containing fifty dollars.

When the Murder Inc. prosecutors brought Elsie in for questioning, she admitted receiving money but knew nothing of the men who took her husband. Well, that was believable, until state's witness Albert "Tick Tock" Tannenbaum told O'Dwyer and Turkus that Elsie was "a liar," and he could prove it.

Possibly one of the first cases of sex, lies, and videotape, Tannenbaum produced a 16mm home movie that blew Elsie's story out of the water. The footage, which was filmed by Tannenbaum, showed Elsie Feinstein – wearing a bathing suit Turkus described as "big as two handkerchiefs" - frolicking on a beach near Miami with Tannenbaum's wife, Jacob "Gurrah" Shapiro and Charles "The Bug" Workman!

Turkus had her re-arrested, saying Elsie had been "an associate of gangsters all her adult life." She of course tried to deny it was her depicted in the film, but after being held in the Women's Detention Center for several months, Elsie decided to cooperate, which won her release. Her husband Sam, well, his body, and that of another missing Murder Inc. victim – Peter Panto, were excavated from shallow graves in New Jersey in May of 1941.

Ruth Sewall

She was a forty-one year old divorcee, mother of a thirteen year old son, living in Brooklyn. Prosecutor's brought her into custody in March of 1940 because they heard she had some sort of *dealings* or *altercation* with members of Murder Inc. The press touted her as being the only person to have defied the mob and lived, following reports she rebelliously marched up to Seymour "Blue Jaw" Magoon and condemned the Combination's demands for a cut of her weekly women's bridge games. Allegedly, Magoon conceded to this, and the boys left her alone.

But, further details emerged that didn't exactly paint Sewall as merely an innocent victim. When the local gangsters learned a fairly worthwhile sum of money was involved in these supposedly-harmless games, well... they wanted their share just like every other gambling joint had to give up. One night after a group of Combination boys marched into Sewall's apartment, tossed the table and threatened her with a knife – she did apparently go straight to Magoon. That part was true enough.

Sewall was questioned for several hours by O'Dwyer's staff, and the story changed dramatically. She completely denied everything to investigators: the bridge games, that any money was exchanged, that she was ever threatened, that she ever sought protection. There wasn't much they could do at that point, so she was released.

Deputy Sheriff William Cassell was found responsible for allowing Vito Gurino's numerous jailhouse visits with witness Joe Liberto. Cassell, accused of also being 'chummy' with Gurino, was consequently forced to resign.

ভ ৵

Chapter 8

The Evil Men Do

"I have an idea the electric chair is going to be working overtime in catching up with justice."

– William O'Dwyer, 1940.

The Murder Inc. trials provided some of the most sensational headlines in crime reporting history. Of the many outlandish and outrageous prosecutions that took place during the early-to-mid 1940's, three in particular received the most notoriety:

Harry "Happy" Maione and Frank "The Dasher" Abbandando, for the murder of George "Whitey" Rudnick in 1937.

Martin "Buggsy" Goldstein and Harry "Pittsburgh Phil" Strauss, for the murder of Irving "Puggy" Feinstein in 1939.

Louis Capone, Emanuel "Mendy" Weiss and Louis "Lepke" Buchalter, for the murder of Joseph Rosen in 1936.

The bulk of evidence used in each of those trials was based on witness testimony, particularly the words of members who turned state's witness. The prosecution basically had their choice of which Syndicate killer to place with which victim because of so many crossovers. Three to five assailants were often present for a single contract job, which meant a lot of these men were involved in a lot of murders. What prosecutors did with respect to that? Sort out which gangster they thought could be deemed most guilty for which murder, then throw them on trial together when possible. This decision was based on the testimony Syndicate squealers had to offer and what the potential jury would hopefully consider was beyond reasonable doubt. The general idea was to put the top killers in the electric chair, not risk having any merely receive life or second degree sentences, so the choices of whom to prosecute for what crime was imperative. For example, Pittsburgh Phil was directly involved and originally indicted with Happy and Dasher in the Rudnick killing, but prosecutors quickly felt his role in the Feinstein murder was more solid, and had a better chance for first degree verdict.

Happy and Dasher

George Rudnick, Whitey they called him, was a lower level guy who dealt in the gambling and loan shark rackets, and thought to be a junky. One day Whitey was seen talking to a police officer, or so Pittsburgh Phil claimed to have observed. Well, that was enough to get the okay from the boss. Whitey knew all the guys – Happy, Dasher, Kid Twist and

Pittsburgh Phil. They were friendly, so luring the mark to his last breath was not going to be very difficult.

Reles paced around and observed the Sunrise Garage, aka "Kaiser Bill's", at 2310 Atlantic Avenue, waiting for Dasher to arrive. Happy Maione instructed "Julie" Catalano to wait across the street, have a drink at Sally's Bar, and not disappear because he would need him later. Happy was juggling responsibilities on the night of May 11, 1937. His grandmother, who lived just down the street, was in the throes of death, but duty for the Syndicate was taking priority. Dasher finally showed up with Rudnick in tow. The pair entered the garage, followed by Reles, Pittsburgh Phil and Happy Maione. Whatever could have been going through Whitey's mind the moment the men converged on him? Minutes later, Reles crossed the street, instructing Catalano to follow him back to the Sunrise. Rudnick's fate was seared into the young associate's mind.

During Maione and Abbandando's trial in May 1940, Catalano delivered testimony even more damning than star witness Reles had provided.

"When I walked into the garage with Abe I saw Harry Maione, Harry Strauss and Abbandando and a stiff laid out on the floor," Catalano began describing the scene. "The Dasher says to me to get the car, so I get the Buick and come back. When I get back the Dasher is dragging the guy by two feet and pulling him into the car. The guy gives out a little cough like this, so Harry Strauss says . . .'the fucking bum ain't dead yet.' So Strauss punches him with the icepick and I seen blood come out of him. Then The Dasher tries to put him in the car, but the guy is too long and don't fit. So Happy Maione says, 'Let me hit the fucker for luck,' and he whacks him one with the meat cleaver."

George "Whitey" Rudnick's autopsy revealed he had been strangled, punctured sixty-three times with an icepick, and struck in the head with a meat cleaver.

Throughout the trial, both defendants tried to display composure during Burton Turkus' naturally sarcastic and relentless character-damaging examination. Maione eventually let his own derisive personality loose, brushing off his attorney's attempt to quell combative retorts, even throwing a glass of water at one point.

Turkus addressed the Reles-led attempt on Meyer Shapiro's life in 1931, querying Maione – "Didn't you supply a .45 automatic and drive the car that time?"

"Reles, the boss, and I supply him?" Happy snarled back.

The examination continued to irk Maione, as Turkus fired off a series of accusations which included other murders, rape, a cross-dressing incident and his infamous threat to all of O'Dwyer's witnesses.

Turkus: On February 6, 1938, when you were dressed as a woman, painted and powdered, didn't you, with others, go into a place and kill two plasterers' helpers?

Maione: I did not.

Turkus: Did you send Gurino out to 'take' Joe the Baker?

Maione: Why don't you ask him that?

Maione was then asked if he and others had once abducted a girl from the Roseland Dance Hall and kept her a prisoner at the Palace Hotel.

"Please don't answer that Maione!" screamed his attorney.

"Why shouldn't I?" Maione brushed off his lawyer's pleas. "But it isn't true."

Frank "The Dasher" Abbandando's turn on the stand was filled with similar queries. His consistent denials of any wrongdoing were augmented by laughs and smiles.

"I never killed anybody in my life," he declared. "He (Reles) is a liar and he knows he lies."

Harry Maione and Frank Abbandando were found guilty of murder in the first degree.

However, the conviction was reversed in January 1941, to which Abbandando said, "What the hell? You don't frame people and get away with it." Maione added (in reference to leaving Sing Sing for retrial in Brooklyn), "I always knew I'd walk out of that tomb."

In April, they received their second conviction, which was upheld the following January. All their hopes were officially extinguished on February 19, 1942, as they were led to Sing Sing's electric chair. Harry "Happy" Maione's last meal was spaghetti and meatballs; Dasher dined on lamb chops.

Buggsy and Pittsburgh Phil

Mafia boss Vincent Mangano wanted the world rid of Irving "Puggy" Feinstein, so he called Albert Anastasia to place the order. The request was honored; Anastasia issued the contract and specifics to Harry "Pittsburgh Phil" Strauss over dinner in September 1939.

"Albert has given the okay," Strauss then told Reles," but wants a clean job."

In other words, the contract issuers wanted nothing left to chance, nothing traceable. Puggy had to disappear. The problem, however, was that none of the boys knew Puggy. His description was given to Strauss, but beyond that... they had little to work with.

A few weeks had passed, Buggsy Goldstein, Kid Twist and Pittsburgh Phil were still pondering the next course of action, and suddenly fate delivered the mysterious Puggy to death's doorstep. It was Labor Day.

Someone from the "extended family" of Syndicate hit men *was* familiar with Puggy Feinstein – Louis "Tiny" Benson, a hulk of a man who was often at Midnight Rose's conducting business with her son Sam Siegel. Tiny and Sam both were into loan, gambling and usury rackets. Puggy, looking for Tiny, strolled up to the candy shop. Once Strauss realized that was their man - a scheme was drawn up on the fly. They told Puggy Tiny wasn't there, but they could take him to where they though he would be. Like an unknowing fly he was led right into the spider's lair.

Abe "Kid Twist" Reles testified, during Goldstein and Strauss's trial, that Puggy was taken to 649 E. 91st Street – Reles' home. He set the stage for Puggy's entrance by first sending his wife and Goldstein's wife out with some money to shop or see a movie (his mother-in-law remained in the home asleep). Puggy arrived with Dukey Maffetore and Buggsy, and almost immediately Strauss and Reles tried to manhandle the victim. Puggy fought back while he was being ice-picked, even biting Strauss's hand at one point. Still, the murderous crew managed to truss Feinstein with rope in such a way that the more he struggled – the more he choked the life out of himself.

Irving "Puggy" Feinstein's body was loaded in a car, dumped in a vacant lot, doused with gasoline and summarily lit on fire. Reles' graphic recounting of the murder and corpse disposal was strengthened even further by the testimony of Anthony "Duke" Maffetore and Seymour "Blue Jaw" Magoon.

"For God's sake, Seymour!" Goldstein screamed. "Tell the truth! Our lives depend on it."

Goldstein and Strauss were not in a good spot, but how each defendant reacted throughout the trial... it was high drama destined for history books, truly some of most outrageous courtroom theater in American history to that point.

Goldstein sobbed, screamed, begged and fidgeted throughout the entire trial. The fear of Old Sparky was clearly seared into his brain from the very start. Reles and Magoon especially caused the gang's once jovial member to turn pale in horror every time they uttered a word on the stand.

Strauss pursued another type of spectacle altogether. Pittsburgh Phil played the "crazy" card. It was performance art at is finest, or perhaps most awful. From June 1st on, he refused to shave.

"I'll keep my beard until trial," Strauss promised. "If I am forced to shave, it will be the same as being forced to testify against myself."

The beard grew in, the coif grew out, and he slimmed down considerably over the next few weeks – appearing gaunt and sickly. He would wear a ratty t-shirt into the courtroom, stare at the ceiling, mumble incoherently and pick his nose periodically. Strauss would tell guards that Abe Reles flew into his cell every night and hid under his bunk. It was priceless entertainment for observers, but the judge, jury and prosecution found neither humor nor sympathy in the act.

On September 20, 1940, jury foreman Walter Woodward delivered the verdict – "We find the defendants... guilty of murder in the first degree."

Goldstein cried. Strauss, still feigning insanity, simply yawned.

Judge John J. Fitzgerald commended the jury for justice being served; assuring them they did the right thing. "There have been eighty-three unsolved murders in Brooklyn," he surmised. "Strauss was involved in twenty-eight, Goldstein in three."

Fitzgerald drew further upon Strauss's history in his final words to the jury. "Not long ago he was going to do a job in Florida. He told his partner the best way would be to kill their victim in a movie house by taking a fire axe from the wall and splitting his skull. Your consciences can rest easy."

The pair were sentenced to death, lost their appeal and were scheduled to die on June 13, 1941. Strauss received two visitors before his death, Evelyn Mittelman and his brother Alex. Goldstein's wife and mother came to say goodbye. Both men ordered steak and chicken for their last meals; Goldstein did not eat, and requested his dinner be given to Maione and Abbandando. Reputedly customary for the weaker of condemned inmates to sit on Old Sparky first, Goldstein walked unassisted, in the company of Rabbi Jacob Katz, to the chamber. Strauss, who remained stoic and silent for weeks, was put to death just minutes after Goldstein. By 11:09 pm – both men gone.

Louis, Mendy and Lepke

Joe Rosen was, for all intent and purpose, a pain in Louis Buchalter's ass. Rosen was in the trucking business, until Lepke pushed him out. But persistence helped get the man back on his feet, as Lepke got him another job in trucking. He lost that job within a year. Finally, the last straw was drawn when Lepke gave a candy store to Rosen. It should have been enough for him and his wife to earn a living, or so the Syndicate boss thought.

Rosen then made the deadly mistake of threatening Lepke Buchalter; Lepke made the deadly mistake of stating, in the presence of a lower level hood, that Rosen was marked for death.

The peaceful morning hours of September 13, 1936, were interrupted by a hail of gunshots. Seventeen slugs had met their mark. Found inside the candy store at 725 Sutter Avenue – the bullet ridden body of Joseph Rosen.

The trial of Capone, Weiss and Lepke may be the most odd, at least in terms of the how it all played out over a four-year span. Lepke was, of course, not present during the murder of candy store owner Joseph Rosen. Louis Capone and Emanuel "Mendy" Weiss were fingered by some of O'Dwyer's singing choir as the director and trigger man. Harry "Pittsburgh Phil" Strauss was said to actually have been a shooter, but he was already out of the picture. Phillip "Little Farvel" Cohen was also indicted. Sholem "Sol" Bernstein, who was mistakenly thought to have been rubbed out, was located and offered to testify against the indicted parties. Stories (unconfirmed and denied years later by O'Dwyer) circulated that even

the mob's most diplomatic member - Frank Costello –
was listed on the indictment.

But Lepke, who surrendered in 1939 after three
years in hiding, was already in federal prison on a
narcotics conviction. Thomas Dewey still wanted him
in New York where he had been convicted for violation
of antitrust laws. Lepke didn't want to face Dewey
again, where he was looking at another thirty years.
Then, O'Dwyer's final puzzle piece was put into place
– the link to what entity actually "ran" Murder Inc.
Lepke was in dire straits.

It was witnesses Albert "Tick Tock" Tannenbaum
and Abe "Kid Twist" Reles who offered testimony
detailing Lepke's issuing the contract on Rosen. The
prosecution was able to finally identify and connect
the literal top guy of the murder division.
Furthermore, Tannenbaum's testimony carried more
weight with the judge and jury than many of the other
killers-turned-witnesses in various trials did. Why?
Allie had nothing to do with the Rosen murder, and
therefore wasn't *perceived* as an accessory who
simply tried pointing the finger elsewhere. There's no
denying the guy was just as guilty as his compatriots
in other Murder Inc. endeavors, but his believability in
Lepke's trial was good enough to help sway the jury to
a guilty verdict for all three defendants in November,
1941. They were sentenced to death in December.

Appeals were filed, and executions were stayed six
times, in a drawn out legal battle between state and
federal authorities. Lepke was still serving time in
Leavenworth – a federal facility. New York demanded

he be sent to Sing Sing. Finally, after a Supreme Court ruling, Lepke Buchalter was turned over to New York in January 1944.

On March 4, 1944, Louis Capone was led the chair. He whispered a prayer. "Mendy" Weiss was brought in next. He stood next to Old Sparky and made one final statement – "I want to say that this was a framed-up case... Governor Dewey knows it."

Louis "Lepke" Buchalter was last. His final statement was not verbal, but rather a note his wife handwrote from his dictation. To the very end – Lepke maintained both his innocence and the ability to have made or destroyed a few unnamed, but well-known politicians. He did not release the information, though it was suggested after his execution that the claim was quite valid. But most of all, Lepke refused to mention, suggest, or implicate any of his Syndicate fellowship.

"Buchalter had two keys in his hand," Lepke's attorney J. Bertram Wegman began the analogy. "He chose to use the one that opened the door to eternity rather than the other one."

Both Mayor LaGuardia and Assistant District Attorney Burton Turkus also commented after Lepke's execution.

"Some people sweated a lot in the last few days," the Mayor said intimating at Lepke's claim of having revealing information on high profile figures.

Turkus added, "He was serving notice to the underworld that he was still 'Lepke the Silent' and if he was talking, he was only involving politicians."

Weaving between the three major Murder Inc. trials were lots and lots of other seedy, strange and shocking happenings; tales of fugitives, faked deaths, mysterious deaths, and, of course, more courtroom antics. Next, meet some of the other unusual players in the murder-for-money drama.

Stories circulated that a woman was present with Maffetore and Goldstein when Puggy Feinstein's body was being disposed of. Allegedly, the unnamed woman offered or requested to light the match that set Puggy's corpse afire, and later bragged about the incident. Harry "Pittsburgh Phil" Strauss's girlfriend – Evelyn Mittelman – was most likely to have been the unidentified female, if the story was true. Mittelman was held as a material witness for a period of time, based on information that convinced Burton Turkus she was much more than a mob moll and knew very detailed inner workings of the murder Combination.

In an effort to help Capone and Weiss avoid the electric chair in 1944, statements were filed from Happy Maione's brother Louis and sister, Jennie Daddona. Maione's siblings told authorities that on the eve of Harry's execution, their condemned brother expressly claimed it was he who was the actual shooter in the Joseph Rosen murder. At first, defense counsel - for Weiss especially – was confident their motions based on that information would save their client. However, it was not enough and all convicted were put to death.

CB EO

Chapter 9

Disappearing Acts

Walter Sage was being *taken for a ride*, but he was the only person in the vehicle unaware of this mortally, a significant fact. He would not have surmised a deadly attack on his health was pending though, simply because he was with his pals, and, on that pleasant late night in July 1937, the crew was heading up to familiar territory – The Catskills. Sage, a Murder Inc. hired gun himself, was also in charge of gambling rackets in the Monticello resort area, so a trip like this was certainly not out of the ordinary.

Seated behind Sage was his closest friend – Irving "Big Gangi" Cohen. Also in the backseat was Jacob "Jack" Drucker, whose family owned a farm near Monticello. Driving the car? That is a mystery still unsolved. Walter Sage was unaware another vehicle was following. Its passengers were Abraham "Pretty" Levine and Harry "Pittsburgh Phil" Strauss.

Conversations carried on for a while; both Cohen and Drucker would periodically lean forward to better chat with the front seat passenger. One of those intimately close moments caused Sage to take his final breath. Each of the backseat occupants brandished icepicks. Cohen leaned in, placed his arm around Sage's neck, thus pulling him tightly against the seat. Drucker then swiftly delivered thirty-two punctures into Sages chest and neck, and even missed once, thereby piercing Cohen's arm. The hapless victim fought hard, grabbing the steering wheel, careening the car into a ditch. And then... the convulsive reaction ceased.

From the scream Cohen made during the erroneous stab, Strauss and Levine were able to locate the murder car in the ditch. As they approached – Cohen was seen sprinting faster than anyone had ever imagined a hulking 240-pound man could possibly do. Drucker, well, he was neatly wiping blood off his icepick. Strauss, though certainly dumbfounded by Cohen's gazelle-like escape into the dark woods, knew there was no time to dwell. A body in a car needed disposing of immediately. Sage's lifeless body was transferred into the follow car and driven to Swan Lake. There the crew did what they thought would make Sage's corpse disappear for good.

First, Sage's body was hogtied and affixed with a rock around the neck. Then, for good measure and probably as a gesture regarding Sage's particular business, the frame of a slot machine was also attached to the body. Sage was tossed into the water and quickly sank. A job well done for a veteran crew of killers? Not exactly.

The murder of Sage was a cut and dry issue for the boys. He'd been skimming from the gambling profits and punishment was ordered. The matter of Irving "Big Gangi" Cohen was a conundrum. Still, regardless of *why* he did it, after fleeing the murder car into the forest, Gangi pretty much earned himself a death sentence, if he didn't already have one. Ironically, that's exactly why Gangi ran in the first place. He believed his own life was next on the chopping block, either because he was involved with killing his own pal and eventually he'd have to 'go' or because he feared Drucker's icepick accident was an intentional strike. Didn't really matter to Big Gangi – he was headed for a name change and new geographic locale.

A little more than two weeks passed when vacationers were shocked out of an otherwise leisurely visit to Swan Lake. Sage's body had surfaced. Strauss, Drucker and Levine knew how to take a life, but they were no experts in the science of decomposition. Once the police removed the remains, Dr. Lee R. Thompkins, coroner, determined the puncture wounds were made while Sage's heart was still pumping blood. What that meant? The blood was filling the numerous tiny entry holes, trapping gasses. Even a rock and a slot machine couldn't hold the body underwater forever once the body became bloated.

Walter Sage was merely one of a number of bodies that turned up in Sullivan County over the last several years. Monticello had been, since 1936 roughly, dubbed by the press as the mob's "Dumping Grounds" or "Gangster's Graveyard." The Sage murder was just another example of gang warfare that probably began in the greater New York City area, yet consistently made its way to the resort outlands. Despite the regularity of discovered bodies – it seemed nobody was able to piece the circumstance together; nobody connected the dots. And for that, men like Drucker and Strauss carried on without much interference.

Big Gangi

The story was far from over. "Pretty" Levine and "Dukey" Maffetore, the first members of Murder Inc. to sing the song of death dealing in early 1940, told District Attorney William O'Dwyer they knew where bodies – the one's the public *didn't* know about - were dumped like garbage, buried and sank throughout the Catskills and surrounding geography. Levine also spoke at length to a grand jury regarding the whereabouts of "Big Gangi" Cohen.

He recalled having some time to kill in fall of 1939, so along with Maffetore, went to the movies. The film was *Golden Boy*. Part way through the picture Levine was astounded by what he saw. Levine quickly nudged "Dukey," seeking to verify what was actually transpiring. There he was – Irving "Big Gangi" Cohen on the silver screen. A bit part, brief appearance, but without a doubt it was him (Cohen acted under the stage name *Jack Gordon*).

Every so often his name would come up in the crew's discourse; basically it was always the then rhetorical question of, "What ever happened to Gangi?" Cohen had made his way to California shortly after the Sage murder. As fate would have it though, Harry "Pittsburgh Phil" Strauss eventually learned of Gangi's general whereabouts (Murder Inc. had associates in Los Angeles, not the least of whom was top boss Benjamin "Bugsy" Siegel). Once the information was confirmed, Strauss ordered Sholem "Sol" Bernstein, a frequent visitor to the West Coast, to find and assassinate Cohen. Sol went to Hollywood alright, but instead of killing Gangi – he got the guy a new gig!

"I went to California to kill Big Gangi," Bernstein admitted in 1941 (while testifying against Louis "Lepke" Buchalter, Louis Capone and Emanuel "Mendy" Weiss - accused in the murder of candy store owner Joseph Rosen). "But I didn't kill him. I had gotten Big Gangi a job as an extra in the movies. I had connections out there."

Bernstein was asked who his connections were, but his defense attorney quickly withdrew the query and instead probed "why?" he frequented California. "You went there on vacation?" he asked.

"Each time I went to California," Bernstein continued, "I went to avoid murder. Don't you call that a vacation."

Like Irving "Big Gangi" Cohen, Sol Bernstein was caught in a web of fear. At any given moment, particularly in the late 1930's when bosses of the Syndicate were becoming increasingly paranoid, any member of the hit squad could find themselves a victim. This was especially dangerous situation for men like Bernstein who were, basically, lower tier associates – car thieves, chauffeurs, and expendable – yet often would bear witness to things that could prove quite damning to upper tier guys.

Now back to 1940. By the time investigators sorted through the "who" involved with Walter Sage's murder, they decided to focus exclusively on the alleged icepick pair. Harry "Pittsburgh Phil" Strauss had already been put on trial for the murder of Irving "Puggy" Feinstein, so bothering with him was of no point, but Cohen and Drucker were fair game.

Police in Los Angeles immediately responded to New York requests to find and apprehend "Big Gangi." Posters and bulletins were passed around the city; it didn't take long to find their man. Cohen was an emotional mess when they grabbed him. Denial, anger, shock, and resistance all formed the bit-part actor's repertoire of post-arrest responses. Cohen's resistance was futile. LA cops prepped him for a journey back to New York where he'd face charges in Sullivan County for the murder of Walter Sage.

The Trial...

On June 17, 1940, Irving "Big Gangi" Cohen sat in court, sobbing intermittently while Abe "Pretty" Levine testified about the night of Walter Sage's murder. Levine went so far as to say he witnessed Cohen help put the body in a truck (which contradicts the version of Cohen running and Sage's body being loaded in the Levine and Strauss follow car.) That's when Gangi wailed aloud – "This man is lying." He covered his teary face with a handkerchief as his wife Eva also began an uncontrollable crying outburst. "I was not there," Gangi argued. "Honest." The scenario was so loud and chaotic the judge called for a short recess so everyone could compose themselves.

When court reconvened, Cohen's counsel, Saul Price, went after Levine, trying to show the witness was no better than his already-convicted counterparts in Murder Inc. Price wanted the jury to consider Levine's role in other murders, such as Irving Ashkenas and Irving "Puggy" Feinstein.

"As far as you know, did Cohen participate in any murder other than the Sage murder?" Price asked.

"No," replied Levine.

"Are you anxious to see Cohen electrocuted for the murder of Walter Sage?" Price continued.

"No," Levine shot back. "I'm not anxious for nothing."

Though a valiant effort to show Levine was merely a self-preserving criminal himself, Price's cross examination didn't seem to have much effect on the actual evidence to that point.

But then…

On June 21st attorney Saul Price gave his closing argument, declaring the prosecution's case against Cohen, "Was insufficient to sustain even a disorderly conduct charge."

Judge Cook explained to the jury that Abraham "Pretty" Levine was an accomplice to the unlawful disposal of Sage's body, and therefore the jurors could disregard his testimony if they believed that testimony was based on Levine receiving immunity. That charge to the jury, along with eight days of Price's effort in court to show Levine was just a gangster, convinced the jury Irving "Big Gangi" Cohen should be set free. The verdict of "not guilty" was read, and Cohen hugged his wife. The pair quietly headed back to California.

Cohen pursued a few more minor roles under several different stage names; one of the last being a bit part on the show *Bonanza*. He passed away in 1976.

Jack Drucker

Jack, like Big Gangi, made himself quite scare shortly following the Sage killing, but he didn't completely disappear just yet. Gangi was in instantaneous danger (or so he justifiably thought), while Drucker was under no immediate duress with the mob or cops, and continued his rackets with the Syndicate, supported his family and, well, buried some bodies here and there. That is until prosecutors began a sweep of Brooklyn bad boys in February and March 1940.

Unlike some of the Murder Inc. trials, such as Maione and Abbandando – Goldstein and Strauss, Cohen was indicted and tried *alone* and *only* for the murder of Walter Sage. Jack Drucker was also indicted separately for the Sage murder, but had an additional three more homicides tacked on: Hyman Yuran, Maurice "Frenchy" Carillot, and Charles "Chink" Sherman. Besides "Pretty" Levine's testimony painting a vivid picture of Drucker cleaning a bloody icepick during Cohen's trial, investigators had reexamined Drucker's suspicious history. The past spoke loudly to his criminal tool kit, which apparently involved the use of quicklime and a shovel. Dating back to the mid 1930's, the Drucker family farm had literally become part of the so-called dumping grounds the press often mentioned. Jack had a habit of disposing dead bodies around and even on the farm property. Still, only in gangland theater could so many obvious and damning elements be overlooked or underestimated.

November 4, 1935...

A carpenter hired to perform some work on the Drucker farm noticed blood on the ground leading to the barn. A call was made and police arrived to discover, first, what appeared to be a partially excavated or incomplete hole near a stone wall on the property. The scene struck them as strange. Besides being an unusual location for random hole, they could see heavy rocks in the opening – scored by spades it appeared, but obviously too difficult to break up. Upon following the blood trail into the barn itself, authorities noticed miscellaneous articles of clothing and an unusually soft spot on the barn floor. Shovels were issued and within minutes the dig revealed a disturbing sight.

Roughly four feet below the barn floor surface were the remains of a human. The pit had been recently dug, but the body was in very bad shape. Quicklime had damaged the victim's skin, and police could see the body had been badly brutalized. Several days after the find, investigators positively identified the victim as Charles "Chink" Sherman – enemy of the late Dutch Schultz. One bullet wound was found in Sherman's arm, but his skull had been hacked by a weapon the coroner figured was an axe.

Sherman had recently been indicted for narcotics trafficking and was offering to be cooperative. Well, word travels fast in the underworld. Despite several police officers keeping an eye on his safety, two men managed to kidnap him outside a cabaret in the city. We know what his fate was.

Even though Sherman's body was found directly on Drucker's father's property, investigators showed little concern for Jack. His prior record was noted, but seemed pretty light by mobster standards so he simply wasn't considered involved. So, who was? At first, the fingers were directly pointed at John "The Fox" Torrio and Charles "Lucky" Luciano – who were vacationing in Florida at the time. Of course the police didn't think either top tier man actually committed the crime, but they were nearly convinced that at least some the men known as the "Big Six" of crime issued the order.

Back to the Sage murder Indictment in 1940...

When Jack Drucker learned of District Attorney William O'Dwyer's office rounding up his pals in droves, that was the signal to disappear permanently. By mid-March 1940 most of the top dogs in the murder division had been picked up, squealers were speaking volumes, and Jack was fingered as a disposal guy. Drucker immediately went into hiding, leaving his wife and young daughter in Brooklyn. Not an unusual move, knowing they'd eventually come for him. It wasn't until May 20th when Sullivan County officials printed off thousands of wanted posters, to be circulated throughout the United States, Canada and Mexico. However, what Drucker did next to vanish and how an innocent family was drawn into the mess... it was the stuff of epic ingenuity and blunder.

Drucker sometimes hid in plain sight, but more often remained out of state. All the while he crafted a plan – one that would be believable in light of common underworld events. He faked his own death. But that's not all. It was clever. Drucker, who hadn't been seen in two years, began spreading rumors throughout the underworld he'd been whacked. And not just killed but that he was tied to a slot machine and dumped in a lake. Yes, just like Walter Sage. Those rumors reached the ears of law enforcement and the news media. The believability was to the degree even a lake was dragged, divers searched and news reports were stating Drucker was *probably* knocked off by the same division he worked for. Jack Drucker's intricate publicity stunt was strong enough to help him stay on the lamb for another year. Good cops don't give up though, and as history shows – criminals sometimes are their own worst enemy.

December 27, 1943...

Police patrolling the Edgemoor Gardens area in suburban Wilmington Delaware spotted a Cadillac bearing New York license plates. The vehicle, they discovered, had been reported stolen only a day before, so State Troopers and FBI were called in. When the authorities entered the home where the car was parked – they found fugitive Jacob "Jack" Drucker. Though surprised, he gave no resistance and admitted the auto theft. With his wife, daughter Sheila and other family members who they had been visiting watching in dismay, Drucker was taken out in cuffs. He was arraigned in federal court, waived extradition and held in a workhouse on $25000 default bail until New York authorities could retrieve him.

However, the ambitious search for one of Murder Inc.'s most elusive was also the cause of much aggravation and distress of another Brooklyn family. During the four years dark haired, gangster Jack Drucker was a fugitive, curly blonde haired Jack Drucker the garment worker was called, investigated, questioned and looked upon suspiciously by the FBI. The non-criminal Drucker was only guilty of happenstance. Along with his wife and child, the law-abiding Jack Drucker lived in a Bronx apartment building at 1972 Walton Avenue, Apt. 3-G. The gangster's wife and daughter... well, they lived in Apt. 2-G!

Shortly after Jack Drucker was apprehended in Delaware, reporters visited the Bronx apartments where *both* Drucker families lived. Jack, the innocent and exhausted Drucker, expressed a soft-spoken sigh of relief as he made his way to work that morning. "Now we can have a little peace and quiet."

As for the icepick-wielding, quicklime and shovel skilled Drucker, he was placed on trial in Sullivan County in May 1944. Though originally indicted for a total of four homicides, he got off easier than many of his nefarious buddies. On May 8th, thirty-nine year old Jacob "Jack" Drucker was found guilty of murder in the second degree for his role in the killing of Walter Sage in 1937. With that, Drucker avoided the electric chair. Several days later he was sentenced from 25 years to life, to be served in Clinton Prison.

There are several listings relating Irving Cohen's film roles on IMDB. Under the name *Jack Gordon* there are two separate entries, same biography, different film resumes for each. Another listing confuses the gangster with famous boxing promoter named Irving Cohen.

The "Big Six" was a term police and press used to distinguish the top organized crime figures in the New York vicinity during the 1930s -1950's. However, the member list varied – depending on what law enforcement or media entity was discussing the topic. Following the murder of Dutch Schultz, Lucky Luciano, Bugsy Siegel, Frank Costello, Jacob Shapiro, Louis Buchalter and John Torrio were labeled as the sextet by some accounts, yet other reports suggested Augie

Pisano and Ciro Terranova were leadership. During the Kefauver hearings in the early 1950's, former District Attorney William O'Dwyer named the 'Big Six' as Luciano, Meyer Lansky, Willie Moretti, Joe Adonis, the late Bugsy Siegel, yet implicitly omitted Frank Costello – which brought much scrutiny because O'Dwyer, then Ambassador to Mexico, was suspected of being quite friendly with Costello over the years.

Wanted posters for Jack Drucker stated the $500 reward was for either information leading to the arrest of Drucker *or* the "finding of his body."

Clinton Prison, located in Dannemora New York, was nicknamed "Little Siberia" for the miserably-cold winters prisoners endured. Charles "Lucky" Luciano also served time in Clinton Prison.

ဆ ၛ

Chapter 10

More Tales of Bad Guys and Dead Guys

The extent of Murder Inc.'s reach was nationwide... *because* it was a tool of the *National* Crime Syndicate. Prosecutors from New York to New Jersey to Detroit to Los Angeles were tallying up victims and reeling in those responsible, as told by the choir of Murder Inc. turncoats. A few of the other trials interspersed among the three most publicized trials were filled with drama, mishaps, and plenty of mysterious happenings.

As with most things in life, there are no guaranteed outcomes. Even the best laid plans are at the mercy of fate and destiny, or judges and juries! A few of the Murder Inc. trials were fraught with less-than-trustworthy witnesses and some truly talented defense attorneys, which did not produce ideal results for the prosecution. Second degree guilt, plea bargains and even some acquittals allowed more than a few killers to ease back into society nearly unscathed.

Max "The Jerk" Golob

John "Spider" Murtha, who had quite a rap sheet himself, was suspected of speaking to police. Lepke ordered a contract. Murtha, while walking down a Brooklyn Street on the morning of March 28, 1935, with girlfriend Florence Nestfield, was approached by two men. Nestfield was asked to "step aside", which she did, and then watched in horror as Murtha was shot to death. Reluctant to come forward at first, Nestfield eventually broke down to prosecutors and named Frank "The Dasher" Abbandando and Max "The Jerk" Golob as the perpetrators.

Abbandando had been tried for the "Whitey" Rudnick murder, which left Max alone to face a first degree charge. But, he caught a big break in February 1942. Florence Nestfield could no longer positively identify "The Jerk" – which forced DA O'Dwyer to reduce the charge. Max took the lower charge and was sentenced to Sing Sing for five years. He was transferred a few months later to Auburn Prison.

Vito "Socks" Gurino

In September 1940, a disheveled, rotund and emotionally unstable man burst through the doors of the Roman Catholic Shrine of the Sea, hysterically screaming, "Three men are gunning for me! I want to see Father Quinn!"

It was Vito Gurino, Murder Inc. gunman who was wanted in connection for multiple murders, and had paid visits to the jail cell of a prosecution witness – all while on the lamb. The man who was once regarded as a feared, heartless killer, nicknamed "Chicken Head" for his preferred method of target practice, had been reduced to tears. Gurino was soon labeled as a "mental zombie" by police and press. Still, he admitted to three murders in hopes of having the prosecution 'save him' from fellow gangsters and the electric chair. He was ultimately convicted in Nassau County for the 1933 murder of John "The Pollack" Bagdonowitz.

Vito then resembled an entirely different man, having shed seventy of those extra pounds. The thinner, yet still emotionally unstable Gurino was sentenced to twenty to life in Sing Sing prison. However, less than a year later it was realized that Gurino was indeed quite crazy, so he was shipped off to Dannemora Hospital for the criminally insane. He died of heart failure in April 1957 at the age of 50.

Jack "Dandy" Parisi

There were lots of "runners" when William O'Dwyer's assault on gangland killers was launched. The one who hid the longest was also the trigger man in Murder Inc.'s most epic fail. When Lepke wanted Philip Orlovsky taken out, Parisi, Seymour Magoon and Jacob "Cuppy" Migden took the assignment. Magoon was the driver. Cuppy's job was to point out the target. The Dandy's duty was pump the mark with enough .38 caliber slugs to satisfy the contract.

Cuppy pointed out the target on the morning of July 25, 1939. Parisi stepped out of the car, drew a pistol and blasted away. Not long after fleeing the scene, the hit squad found out they killed the wrong man. Irving Penn was a classical music publisher, family man and had absolutely nothing to do with the mob. But, Penn resembled the intended target. The blame game had begun, but it was irrelevant by that point. The Murder Inc. crackdown inspired both Cuppy and Parisi to flee.

Cuppy had some plastic surgery, hid in St. Louis, but still got nabbed first. Pleading guilty to attempted assault in the first degree in 1943, he was given a five-year sentence, and faded from the headlines and notoriety thereafter.

Parisi remained in hiding for ten years. He was grabbed by police in Pennsylvania in 1949 and put on trial in 1950 for the Penn murder, which ended in acquittal. After returning to his home and business (a dress manufacturing company) in Hazelton Pennsylvania (where he'd been all along), Parisi was again arrested in 1953. Immigration tried to deport him based on a 1926 dope arrest he had served time for. Dandy fought the deportation with success. He died in 1982 at the age of 83.

Irving "Knadles" Nitzberg

He was the Combination's man-in-the-Bronx. Knadles, who was also known as "Kay," took the job of rubbing out Albert "Plug" Shuman in January 1939. Lepke worried Shuman spoke to cops and Knadles knew the victim well, so it was good choice. Shuman was taken for a ride, shot twice in the head. As was generally the course of action though, Nitzberg was certainly not the only man involved in the plot.

Abe Reles testified that a whopping "eight" Murder Inc. members planned or participated in the hit. Reles named Mendy Weiss, Morris "Shep" Shapiro (a fugitive who was never located), Charles "The Bug" Workman, Samuel "Tootsie" Feinstein, Albert Tannenbaum and Seymour "Blue Jaw" Magoon, and Harry "Pittsburgh Phil" Strauss. Nitzberg was the only one convicted. He was sentenced to death in 1941, but amazingly avoided a trip to Old Sparky - thanks to two overturns and the mysterious death of a star witness.

How did his life turn out? Well, it wasn't quite ten years later when Knadles was picked up for bond theft. His return to crime didn't stop there either. He again made the news in 1963 when he was netted in a loan shark conspiracy.

Benjamin "Bugsy" Siegel

The dapper, wannabe movie star, was not only a founding member of the National Crime Syndicate, but he was one of the very few top bosses who actually conducted some hands on work. Yes, Bugsy was the kind of gangster who could and did carry out violent resolve, personally.

In another of Lepke's stoolpigeon purges of 1939, Harry Greenberg was slated for death. Big Greenie, once very close with guys like Siegel, Lepke and Gurrah Shapiro, had made the fatal mistake of issuing threats to the Syndicate. Lepke had Murder Inc. henchman chasing Greenberg around the country, always arriving at locations just a little too late. That is... until he was found in Los Angeles living under the alias "Schacter" with his wife Ida.

The job was assigned to Albert "Tick Tock" Tannenbaum, to be overseen by Siegel – who had been in California for a number of years on the Syndicate's behalf. Also told to participate was "Sol" Bernstein, but he was allegedly a 'no show' which of course earned him a death sentence. Bugsy Siegel initiated a backup plan, bringing in "Whitey" Krakower and Frankie Carbo for the gig. Both men, trusted old pals of Siegel, were heavily involved in boxing, fight fixing and other criminal exploits.

Greenberg arrived at his house on the night of November 22, and while seated in his car, was shot multiple times in the head. His wife Ida discovered the bloody scene after hearing what she thought was a vehicle backfiring.

Bugsy Siegel, Benjamin Krakow, Harry "Champ" Segal and Carbo were indicted in 1940. Bugsy and Carbo were named by Albert Tannenbaum, who was the driver of a distraction vehicle during the hit on Greenberg. Los Angeles prosecutors requested Abe Reles and Tannenbaum be sent to California to testify. At first, William O'Dwyer was reluctant to ship his star witnesses out of New York, but eventually agreed. Well, even after the two witnesses identified and detailed how Carbo shot Greenberg and Siegel was the man in charge, curiously, Bugsy and Carbo's indictments were dropped in December. Bugsy's story wasn't over yet, but something happened, almost a year later, that altered the course of Murder Inc. prosecutions...

A Twist of Fate...

At 6:45 pm on the night of November 11, 1941, a clerk on the night shift of the Half Moon Hotel in Coney Island heard a loud thud coming from outside on an extension roof. He did not investigate, thinking it was probably garbage being incinerated. He was incorrect in that assumption.

The hotel was where Abe "Kid Twist" Reles and several of the other "singers" were being lodged. Although the witnesses were under heavy guard at all times, somehow Abe Reles dropped six stories to his death. The biggest Murder Inc. related mystery of all – how did Kid Twist really end up on that extension roof? It looked, at first, like he had tried to lower himself with bedding and wire, but his weight was too much stress on the improvised rope. Theories abound, investigations rampant, arguments over who was at fault. Was he pushed? Thrown? Did he try to escape? Suicide? The possibility he was simply playing a practical joke on guards was raised.

There are some incredibly well researched books and articles that focus specifically on the details and possibilities surrounding Reles' death, for which nobody was ever prosecuted. It's a subject likely to be discussed and debated for many years to come, but Burton Turkus certainly believed it was no suicide. The incident would haunt William O'Dwyer for years to come, as he faced criticism and condemnation for that fiasco and other questionable incidents during the Murder Inc. era.

Consequence of a Dead Rat...

Reles had been key in securing the convictions of his fellow gunslingers. He put the screws to Lepke Buchalter – a feat even Lepke never imagined could be achieved. The star squealer had survived in spite of all that. But then came DA O'Dwyer's much anticipated prosecution plan – go after the other boss of Murder Inc.

Kid Twist's death occurred the day before he was scheduled to testify against Albert Anastasia, aka Lord High Executioner, aka The Mad Hatter. That dynamic, paired with the impending re-indictment of Benjamin "Bugsy" Siegel, was as good a reason as any for even a well-protected witness to be silenced, somehow. Because Reles never made the date with Anastasia, and because he was unable to resume testimony in Bugsy's second trial the following year – both top mob bosses were free as the wind.

Sholem "Sol" Bernstein, at first, couldn't be found during William O'Dwyer's search mission for Murder Inc. members. Of course the initial thought from investigators was that Sol met his maker for ditching Bugsy Siegel's mission to assassinate Harry Greenberg. That concern was amplified when authorities in Chicago discovered a burlap sack containing the severed torso and legs of a man. Police were fairly convinced it was the remains of Bernstein, but later that month Sol appeared alive and well, subsequently placed in protective custody by William O'Dwyer's staff.

Beside the Harry Greenberg murder indictment, Siegel was indicted for "harboring a fugitive" (Buchalter). Abe Reles also testified that he and Bugsy Siegel met with then-fugitive Louis "Lepke" Buchalter in a Brooklyn safe-house. Siegel's alibi was based on documentation he had been in Europe on the date Reles claimed they visited Lepke. Siegel stated in court that he "knew" Lepke because they grew up in the same neighborhood. "As for this guy," Siegel stated of Reles, "I never saw him until he appeared in court, here."

80 03

Chapter 11:

Facts, Folklore and More

The Murder Inc. era was undeniably the most unusual and heinous period in the history of the American mob's existence. The perpetrators were many, and to the dismay of society as a whole – able to operate with little interference for an entire decade. Men who lived and breathed the gangster lifestyle were commonplace. The ones who were capable of thrusting an icepick 50 times into another human being – a complete stranger or close companion having zero relevance once a contract was issued – were of an entirely unique ilk.

The dismantling of the latter did not put an end all mob sanctioned violence, obviously. It did however expose and pull the plug on the most unusual, complex, violent and long-running singular grouping of individual killers the American underworld had ever produced. There was nothing like it before; nothing like it since. In the eyes of the law, the most evil of the tight-knit group were put to death, never to wreak such havoc in the world again. So in those terms – the work was a success. But do stories like this ever really end? And, where did some begin?

One can imagine how many "other" things happened to shape the Murder Inc. crewmembers, or what other crimes the committed? And then there's the ultimate question... *Did they aspire to such reputations all along?*

The following is a collection of little facts, rumors, legends, reports and quotes. Perhaps these little tidbits from the past will offer more insight into vast and unbelievable lives of mob's most deadly hit squad.

Interesting Quotes

July 1931, Magistrate George M. Curtis of Brooklyn Homicide Court – disgusted at having to dismiss Abe Reles, Frank Abbandando and Harry Strauss – said, *"Possibly a vigilance committee will be formed and start to hang some of these people from lamp posts."*

April 1932, same three defendants found not guilty by a jury, which drew the ire of Judge Franklin Taylor. Upon regretfully dismissing the trio, he commended the arresting police officers for their efforts, adding, *"Gentlemen, you have to let three killers go."*

March 1934, Harry Maione in court for a robbery charge – not a single witness could identify him. Magistrate Sabbatino responded by addressing the court stenographer directly, so his statement would be clearly recorded. *"I know this man Maione to be a* mobster, a gangster, and a murderer, but I can't prove it."

October 1934, Abe Reles was acquitted in the murder of garage attendant Alvin Snydor. The presiding judge addressed the shocking verdict by predicting Reles would probably be killed by police in the near future anyway. *"No cop can kill me,"* Reles snarled back. *"A cop has to count to ten before he can fire his gun."*

November 1934, Police Commissioner Lewis Valentine addressed a staff of police officers, regarding Harry "Pittsburgh Phil" Strauss. *"This man is a paid assassin. Men like him should be marked up and mussed up. Blood should be smeared all over that velvet collar. Instead, he looks like he just got out of a barber's chair."*

August 1937, Abe Reles and Martin "Buggsy" Goldstein were arraigned on vagrancy charges. Goldstein said he was gainfully employed as a clerk. Reles describe himself as a "Soda Jerk." Magistrate Solomon commented, *"I don't know about the soda, but I know he's a jerk."* Nevertheless, the judge was forced to dismiss them, regretfully adding - *"They have money, and they have homes, and they are always able to make bail. Under the law, there is nothing we can do."*

February 1938, Louis "Tiny" Benson was arrested - on a vagrancy charge with Joseph Bernstein and Harry "Pittsburgh Phil" Strauss's younger brother Alex – who tried to mimic Phil's suave fashion sense and criminal resume. In light of not having quite the criminal record of his companions, Benson- a 420 lbs. behemoth - joked to the arresting officers, *"The reason you boys don't pick me up much is there ain't no room in the wagon for me."*

April 1940, *"They had no hearts; they were positively cruel,"* said William O'Dwyer of the two Murder Inc. members he found most despicable. *"Strauss and Happy were bloodthirsty and stopped at nothing."*

April 1940, the blame game began; who or what was responsible for producing such a criminal enterprise as Murder Inc.? Milton J. Goell, Chairman of the Brooklyn Committee for Better Housing professed his answer to the problem - *"Slums in the Brownsville area will continue to spawn gangsterism and such combines as Murder Inc. until these slums are wiped out and replaced by some form of public housing within easy reach of the low-income brackets."*

May 1940, under cross-examination by Burton Turkus, Frank "The Dasher" Abbandando would admit only to having been a lowly bookie. *"Did you get the name Dasher while you were earning ten dollars a week?"* the smarmy prosecutor asked. *"No,"* replied Abbandando, *"While I was playing ball in 1933... in prison."*

June 1940, Judge George W. Martin heard the plea of Buggsy Goldstein's attorney, requesting his client to be tried separately from Harry Strauss. During the arguments, star witness for the prosecution (and subject of much controversy) – Abe Reles - was mentioned, to which Martin declared, *"I think he's a yellow dog. I am the only one ever to have sent him to prison."*

December 1951, Burton Turkus, aka Mr. Arsenic – who had gone on to host a television show, pen columns and the definitive book covering Murder Inc. – referred to (with his innate sarcasm) the women involved in Syndicate affairs as the "Ladies Auxiliary of Murder Inc." In one of his syndicated articles offered this characterization - *"Mostly, the Ladies Auxiliary of Murder Inc. consisted of girlfriends –clinging, curvaceous clothes-horses with fur and diamonds and the lacquered look of store-window mannequins."*

Anecdotes

Sam "Dapper" Siegel

Drama Queen...

In 1939 he fainted his way into the news upon learning his dear old mother – Midnight Rose Gold – was indicted for perjury. Well, Dapper must've had acting in his blood, because that incident wasn't the first time he tried his hand at the dramatic arts. Back in August 1936 an occurrence outside Midnight Rose's store gave Sam the opportunity to put on a show that trumped his feigned-faint spectacle. Buggsy Goldstein, Louis Capone, Blue Jaw Magoon and a few other hangarounds had been getting a bit rowdy inside the store, which drew the attention of patrolman Edward Spaeth. He, in plainclothes at the time, was joined by another patrolman and the pair entered the store.

They frisked five men and charged them all with disorderly conduct. That's when Sam's showmanship kicked in; he ran into the street – frantically screaming he was "being held up."

The following day, Patrolman Spaeth, probably shaking his head in dismay, explained to the magistrate that, plainclothes or not, Sam Siegel and he knew each other well. The judge dismissed five of the defendants for lack of evidence, but Siegel's performance netted a $25 fine.

Harry "Happy" Maione

Love Affair...

The majority of Murder Inc. brethren were family men, wives, children, pets – they appeared to have it all. Pittsburgh Phil wasn't married, but kept steady company with Evelyn Mittelman for a straight five years. Harry "Happy" Maione was among the few true bachelors of the lot. Very little was ever reported of Happy's love life. So then, did he have one? According to an interesting tale offered by author Michael Gourdine – Happy crossed the racial barrier with at least one love interest. He recalls his fraternal grandmother – Helen Gourdine – sharing stories with the family about her personal history and experience with Harry Maione.

"She talked about *Murder Incorporated* like they were the most respected men on earth," says Gourdine. "Back during the Great Depression she was a teenage prostitute in Sugar Hill Harlem. She returned to Brooklyn in her 20's where she met Harry Maione."

Gourdine says his grandmother enjoyed recounting the time of her affair with Happy Maione literally until the day she died. "She talked about the glory days in Brownsville Brooklyn, at this time I believe she lived in East New York. She bragged about how other blacks weren't allowed to visit the "Candy Store" but she was...where all the "Big Shots" would be inside wearing expensive suits."

Gourdine remembers Helen having spoken of Happy's hair, or rather – how much Happy attended to his coif. Besides the memories of romance with Maione and having been inside the infamous Midnight Rose's, Helen told her grandson the highlight was having met the Boss.

"She actually got to meet "Judge Louie" -Louis Buchalter," Gourdine says. "This was a big deal for a black person from Brooklyn."

After the major Murder Inc. trials finished, and Harry Maione was put to death, Gourdine says Helen moved in with her sister in a different part of town. A few years later she became pregnant (with Michael's father), and began a brand new chapter of her life. Helen Gourdine passed away on June 18, 2008.

Dons a Dress...

In early 1939, a contract was put on two plasterers, Cesare Lattaro and Antonio Siciliano. The pair had been ordered to 'take out' a fellow plasterer that was causing trouble for the union. Apparently the men chose *not* to do as instructed, which of course earned them the death warrant. The board of Brooklyn hit men convened, discussed, and ultimately concluded the job was a potentially problematic hit. However, in light of Lattaro and Siciliano's reputation - *Lotharios* and *playboys* - a clever plan was hatched to woo the marks into an easy kill. Harry Maione was the perfect choice for an assignment that required, well, a distinctly feminine touch. Maione, who was of considerably smaller stature than most of his cohorts, underwent a gender transformation; clothing, makeup, false eyelashes, the works (Vito Gurino's wife Gertrude provided the female accoutrements).

Some reports stated the men believed they had been set up on a blind date, in February 1939, and thereby had no hesitation opening their basement apartment door for a pretty lady caller. Contrasting stories describe the men as having been sound asleep, not necessarily expecting their date's arrival. Regardless of the scenario, the plasterers did allow entry to what they believed was a woman. Maione, dressed in drag, with a gun concealed inside a fur wrap, entered the dwelling. "Socks" Gurino and "Dasher" Abbandando then appeared from the shadows and together they fired a dozen rounds into the room. The bullet-riddled bodies of Lattaro, Siciliano and, sadly, their bulldog, were found a day later.

Ostentatious Obsequies...

On February 24, 1942, over 700 mourners, thirty-six police officers and four photographers were present at the Maione home on 177 Rockaway Avenue. Harry "Happy" Maione's funeral was truly fit for a king. Five vehicles adorn with $1000 worth of flowers were lined behind a chime-playing high-end hearse; Maione's body was carried out in a $3000 dollar bronze casket. Though known for his eternal scowl, eagerness to fight, and skill in a twisted career of bloodlust – his interment was an affair rivaling that of any top ranking or highly respected Syndicate boss or Mafia Don.

The spectacular procession followed Happy to the Our Lady of Loreto church on Pacific and Sackman streets. Following the services, he was buried in St. John's Cemetery in Queens – the final resting place for many of New York's infamous gangsters. All the while, the dozens of police kept a close eye on the crowds; they didn't want a repeat of the previous day. "Dasher" Abbandando's funeral was disrupted by a heated exchange between a sibling and the press. Dasher's younger brother Rocco was arrested after he charged Henry W. McCallister, a photographer for the New York Journal-American. Rocco, unlike his brother, had no criminal record until he became irate at what he perceived as invasion of privacy. "I didn't want to kick him," he claimed during his lineup for felonious assault. "I was aiming at the camera. I didn't want pictures of my family in the papers."

On May 16th, Rocco caught a break. Prosecutor Burton Turkus suggested a lesser charge of disorderly conduct, to which Abbandando agreed and plead guilty. He shook hands with the photographer he assaulted and the judge issued a suspended sentence.

Vito Gurino

Head Case...

He was called "Torpedo, Chicken Head and Socks," throughout the underworld, but police and prosecutors had another label for him in 1940 – insane. In a little known cranially-related incident dating back to February 1934, Gurino had his skull fractured during a mysterious melee that broke out in a beer garden establishment at #699 Ralph Avenue in Brooklyn. When police arrived they found Gurino on the floor, bleeding heavily, and a bartender who claimed he knew nothing of the incident particulars. Gurino was taken to Unity Hospital, but he was arrested shortly thereafter, as was Harry "Happy" Maione on the charge of robbery. According to the beer garden's proprietor – Herman Levine – two or three men tried to rob the tavern and a fight broke out. Gurino's charge was dismissed by Judge Algeron Nova later that month. Maione was brought before Judge Sabbatino in March. His indictment raised the ire of Sabbatino (see the "quotes" section) because detectives did not have any supporting evidence against Maione. The only witness, tavern owner Herman Levine, suddenly refused or was unable to identify Maione as a perpetrator of the attempted robbery and subsequent brawl.

Dog lover?

Gurino was a recognizable character around the Ozone Park area for two reasons. The first - he was a very large and, as some referenced him, slovenly. Hard to miss the gargantuan tough guy. Secondly, he was regularly seen walking or 'parading' his two Scottie dogs. A real softie in an oversized frame? Not quite. Following his nervous breakdown and surrender to authorities during the Murder Inc. roundups, Gurino's role in the Siciliano and Lattaro murders was detailed a little further. The image of a canine loving Gurino was disintegrated when information revealed he was actually the killer of the plasterers' dog – further stripping his reputation and any remote possibility of sympathy – from mobsters, the press or public.

"There is no incident where a gunman harmed a pet. Somehow, that way they are weak – or, perhaps, human," wrote columnist Clifford Evans of Gurino breaking a gangland rule. He went on to detail the entire murder scene, closing with a heartbreaking tone – "The dog wouldn't leave his pals. No bigger than a lap-dog, he jumped at the men who had killed his friends. But the same guns that killed Siciliano and Lattaro pumped bullets into the dog. That little added touch was Gurino's."

Harry "Pittsburgh Phil" Strauss

Sobriquet...

Strauss was known by two nicknames: *Pittsburgh Phil* and *Pep*. The latter was preferred by his close friends within the Combination and, as nicknames often are, was probably laid upon him by those very friends. The former? The origins have been debated for many decades. It is very likely Strauss adopted "Pittsburgh Phil" from a well-known gambler of the late 1800's named George E. Smith. The original "Pittsburgh Phil" was in the press quite a bit, often called a "plunger" – old term for a reckless gambler. Despite the media's feelings for Smith, there was no denying the man went into the gambling history book as one of the most successful bettors. Smith was still being lauded for his ability to make bookies "pay and pay and pay" until the day he died in 1905. It was estimated his gambling profits were around three-million dollars, which was left to his heirs. Harry Strauss, by most accounts, was definitely quite fond of his own developing reputation, so taking on an ostentatious identifier would have been nothing short of expected. Harry relished attention.

Researchers and historians have also explored the possibility of Harry Strauss picking up the nickname from some connection to actual city of Pittsburgh Pennsylvania. Although he was known to be among the more prolific Murder Inc. members, of whom were trusted with national business trips, solid data to either confirm or deny he was ever in the Steel City did not materialize. With one exception -

Shortly after the murder Syndicate story went viral in early 1940, one newspaper in particular thought to delve into Harry Strauss's possible relationship to the city of Pittsburgh. The Pittsburgh Press ran a syndicated UP article on Murder Inc. on March 22,

1940 titled *Women Provide Key to Killing.* The Press also inserted a fragment of their investigative work into the story:

"Pittsburgh police have no record of a Pittsburgh Phil Strauss. Although in July 1927, a man arrested with five others on suspicion of an auto theft, gave 'Harry Strauss' as one of his aliases. This man, later released, gave a Brooklyn address."

Again, it seems more likely Strauss borrowed his alias from the late gambler. However, if he was in fact the same Harry Strauss picked up by Pittsburgh Police in 1927 – the opportunity to have acquired such a moniker at that time, (considering the infinite ways in which people find themselves tagged with curious nicknames) is not outside the realm of theoretical possibility.

Speaking of Pittsburgh...

Donald MacGregor penned an article titled "America: Zoned for Crime," which ran on June 30, 1940, and was based on information supplied by Henry F. Guggenheim – President of the Citizens' Committee on the Control of Crime in New York, Inc. Guggenheim's organization produced a map illustrating how they believed the United States was divided and controlled by major gangsters such as Louis "Lepke" Buchalter and Jacob "Gurrah" Shapiro. Pittsburgh was considered a major hub.

AMERICA'S CRIME CITIES	
ATLANTIC CITY:	Gambling, robbery.
BALTIMORE:	Gambling, robbery.
CHICAGO:	"Protection" rackets, robberies.
DETROIT:	Robbery, gambling.
HOT SPRINGS:	Fence city for securities.
JERSEY CITY:	Robbery, gambling.
KANSAS CITY:	Gambling, rackets.
LOS ANGELES:	No. 1 city for gambling.
NEW ORLEANS:	No. 2 city for gambling.
NEW YORK:	Shakedown rackets, robberies.
NEWARK:	Robbery, gambling.
PHILADELPHIA:	meeting center for racketeers.
PITTSBURGH:	Robbery, gambling.
ST. LOUIS:	Haven city for gangsters.
WASHINGTON:	Gambling, robbery.

Hit and Didn't Run...

While cruising along Kings Parkway on the evening of November 8, 1937, Pittsburgh Phil's car struck seventy-five year old pedestrian Clara Mittleman. What did the normally heartless killer do? What any otherwise righteous citizen would – he tried to assist her and then called the cops. Unfortunately the victim died on scene, which meant Phil had to face charges. His attorney, Leon Fischbein, requested $1000 bail, saying – "This fatal accident was an unfortunate occurrence. It happened to Strauss; it could have happened to Judge Malbin."

"Do me a favor," the judge responded. "Do not compare me with Mr. Strauss, please. $2500 bail."

Martin "Buggsy" Goldstein

Climbing the Corporate Ladder...

When Buggsy Goldstein and Pittsburgh Phil Strauss found out they were wanted in connection with the 1935 double-murder of Morris Kessler and Joseph Amberg, they took their lawyer's advice and turned themselves into police. As Police Captain Frederick Zwirz was putting the men in lineup, Buggsy fired off a commentary that essentially answers the million dollar question about these gangsters – How did they see themselves?

"The papers list me as Public Enemy number 6," said Buggsy to the Captain. "That's a lousy rating. I worked hard and I hope to get a better rating than that."

By 1937, Buggsy and pals had been paraded through morning lineups at police stations so many times; one would think they were complacent with the ritual. However, and in sync with the boastful Buggsy quote, police began to find the veteran criminals rather "bashful" during the near-routine visits. Goldstein and Reles in particular were growing ashamed and/or tired of the frequency, or so the police seemed to think. Most of what the pair loathed about the lineups – being referred to by the lowly term "punks."

Abe "Kid Twist" Reles

Killer name?

The origin of Reles' nickname has been attributed to several things; the candy, his preferred method of murder, and in homage to another Brooklyn gangster - Max "Kid Twist" Zweifach. Well, the theories might be debated for eternity, but 'method of murder' can probably be ruled out – if Reles' own testimony is to be believed. During the trial of Buggsy Goldstein and Pittsburgh Phil, he confessed to at least eleven personally-committed murders, but noted the first time he ever used that particular method of murder was on Irving "Puggy" Feinstein in 1939. He had been known as "Kid Twist" for several years prior to that murder.

An article by Robert Musel, which ran in March 1940, stated Reles' wife told prosecutors her husband had indeed admired the gangster Max Zweifach. Moreover – at the Reles house – she was expected to call Abe by the moniker "Kid Twist" and their son was known as "Little Kid Twist."

It's Not Business, It's Just Personal...

Reles is considered by many experts on the history of Murder Inc. as the worst, sickest and/or most violent of the entire bunch. That sentiment was shared by those who questioned and opposed DA William O'Dwyer's decision to use Reles as their star witness, and had he lived, possibly gotten off pretty unscathed. One of the many examples of Reles' brutality was levied upon two black men who, by all accounts, were not marked for any mob contract, but simply were at wrong place, wrong time, and happened to be engaged by a hot-tempered Reles.

In the early morning hours of February 15, 1934, Charles Battle, an attendant working at a garage on 110 East 98th street, was beaten over the head with a bottle. The perpetrators, Abe Reles and Harry Strauss had apparently taken offense to something Battle said or did. The story was reported with slightly different versions. One account stated Battle was investigating a ruckus the gangsters were making in or around the garage and the men attacked him. Another version stated Reles was impatient with the speed of service and a fight broke out. Regardless of circumstance, Reles held Battle and Strauss hit him with a bottle.

Both men fled the scene, but the evening assaults were far from over. Reles returned. Why? Apparently to finish off Battle. However, Charles Battle had been long gone by then, tending to his injury. To the great misfortune of another attendant – Alvin Sydnor – Reles wasn't checking identification. Sydnor was beaten and stabbed in the back. Battle testified against Reles during the first indictment, but by the time Reles was being tried for the Sydnor murder, neither Battle nor another witness – William Lee – had seen the actual stabbing. Further, the case was dragged out for another year and by that point – both witnesses had made themselves scarce. The court assumed the witnesses were in fear of intimidation or retaliation. In the end, Reles did in fact serve some jail time, but the original "felonious assault" charge was lowered to a third degree charge. In other words, once again Reles was back on the street in short order.

Both Strauss and Reles had numerous court appearances. And even though Reles actually got jail time for the incident, it was laughable. The original 'felonious assault' charge was lowered, and two original witnesses – Charles Battle and another attendant,

STD?

One of the many predictions made of Reles' bleak future outlook appeared in the November 19, 1940 edition of New York PM Newspaper. Besides forecasting the obvious dangers Reles was facing as a star prosecution witness, the article revealed a medical condition:

"Reles is a 4-Plus syphilitic. And if that doesn't kill him, if he goes free or gets a light sentence, then one of his old gang probably will."

The 4-Plus rating refers to the Wassermann Test - a 1906 discovery of an antibody test for Syphilis. If the PM article's assertion was true, it meant Kid Twist was in the most severe stage of neurosyphilis by the time he was taking the stand against all his former cohorts.

However, the suggestion that Reles was afflicted with the same disease that Al Capone suffered from –

Paresis – was dismissed by Assistant District Attorney Edward Silver during the 1951 probe of Reles' mysterious death.

Rat, literally...

As Abe Reles' funeral came to a close, one individual amongst the small group of attending mourners spotted a small animal dart across the landscape. "It's a gopher," the voice said. "The rat is in the grave."

The Reles' Gang

Dope Men...

Something that still seems to be a bit hazy in the public perception of mob vice regards *narcotics*. Yes, the mob and the Mafia did in fact traffic narcotics dating all the way back to at least 1914 when the Harrison Act sought to limit cocaine and heroin to medical use only. By 1923, both drugs were officially illegal. Gangsters were not limiting themselves to bootlegging liquor; prohibition meant dope as well.

Charles "Lucky" Luciano was arrested more than once on possession charges beginning in his teenage years, Arnold Rothstein employed an entire staff of skilled importers and traffickers in the 1920's, and Louis "Lepke" Buchalter was federally indicted for his role in narcotics trafficking in 1937. Dope was a lucrative vice. The Brownsville and Ocean Hill crews were tapped into rackets across the board – dice, slots, liquor, prostitution, shylock, and of course – illicit drugs. Although narcotics was certainly not the crew's primary area of interest, the burgeoning unification under Reles' leadership was nailed in 1932 during a drug sting operation conducted throughout Brooklyn. Police entered the back room of a bootblack shop at 1754 East New York Avenue, and found eight Reles gang members present, along with a vile of morphine. Abe Reles, Harry and Louis Maione, Vito Gurino, Angelo "Julie" Catalano, Louis Sica, Alfred Mercuri and Harry "Pittsburgh Phil" Strauss were all arraigned on possession charges. They were all subsequently discharged, not surprising.

Horrible Employees...

The real troubles these otherwise-reliable gangsters presented in their resumes should have thrown up red flags back to the mid 1930's. Long before the obvious mess created for Syndicate bosses when Murder Inc. thugs began turning state's witness in 1940, the notorious Reles Gang had seedy extracurricular activities that perhaps showed their collective true colors. Abe Reles himself was mockingly dubbed a "Great Lover" in 1934 following an arrest for "flirting" and "molesting" two girls on a street corner. Then, in 1937, the entire Reles Gang was being investigated for an abduction of a schoolgirl. The only witness, eighteen year old Anna Rosenblum, was threatened with the warning – "If you don't testify right, your body will be found in the gutter." The kidnapped girl's parents were offered a $1000 bride to remain silent, which they did not accept. Nevertheless, all eight suspects were freed when none of the victims would positively identify anyone in court.

In 1940, a seventeen-year-old singer came forward to Burton Turkus and shared her story, which entailed abduction, rape and attempted-bribery. In the singer's case, Harry Maione, Vito Gurino and Frank Abbandando were specifically named as the perpetrators. It should be noted - there are some discrepancies and/or mystery regarding the numerous abduction accusations. Turkus questioned Maione in court of kidnapping the girl from the Roseland Dancehall and kept her hostage at the Palace Hotel. However, in other reports of the testimony, Turkus spoke of a girl they allegedly abducted in Queens County in 1939, assaulted in an automobile, and was then thrown back into the street. None of the victims' names were released by the DA's office, for obvious reasons. In any case, the many instances of non-Syndicate-related activities, particularly against minors and innocents, should have shown the bosses these guys were not nearly as disciplined or reliable as they may have once thought.

The Purple Gang

Out of Towners

Around the same time New York prosecutors realized Detroit Purple Gang member Izzy Burnstein had come to town with Syndicate boss Bugsy Siegel (in April 1940), they had gathered further information – from their stable of informants and turncoats – that Motown had been paid a visit by Brooklyn's baddies in 1937. Harry Millman, a boisterous Purple Gang hood and former Abe Burnstein bodyguard, had, as rumors suggested, made enemies from both his Jewish gangster brethren and the Italian Mafia in the Detroit region. Well, that wasn't very smart on Millman's part. "After Prohibition and the Purples' disbandment (Abe's retirement)," explains author Scott Burnstein, "Millman had a difficult time and fought coming under the Italian LCN umbrella in Detroit."

First, his car was bombed in the summer of 1937. Harry wasn't in it, but one of his cohorts was blown to bits. Millman wised up enough to only go out in crowds, never allowing himself in a "lone" and vulnerable state. That however did not matter much on Thanksgiving night. While eating and boozing at Boesky's restaurant and delicatessen, Millman was approached by two unfamiliar men. They quickly pumped nine bullets into Millman, hit a few bystanders in the process, and then simply strolled back out of the establishment.

Detroit police found a vehicle believed to be the getaway car – stolen, with New York plates. Though Detroit authorities worked closely with New York during the investigation, nothing much materialized. "They must have been strangers to the city," was the theory suggest by Henry Piel, Chief of Detectives. "Local gangsters wouldn't have gone about the job in such a bold way."

The alleged assassins were not revealed by name until the Murder Inc. prosecutions began in 1940. The tale shared with William O'Dwyer's staff pointed directly to a couple of top tier Syndicate killers. "Millman was killed on a contract farmed out to NY's

Murder Inc.," Burnstein adds. "And carried out by "Happy" Maione and "Pittsburgh Phil" Strauss."

Louis "Lepke" Buchalter

Surrender

More than a few stories circulated as to *how* and *who* was involved, exactly, when Louis "Lepke" Buchalter made the decision to surrender in 1939. A 1975 Miami News article by Dennis Eisenberg, Uri Dan and Eli Landau addressed the version told by Joseph "Doc Stacher" Rosen.

"It was (Meyer) Lansky," said Rosen of who convinced Lepke's closest remaining pal, Moe Wolensky, to basically trick the fugitive to give himself up.

"We had made our mind up that the days of shooting people were over," Rosen explained. "We worked out a plan and Lepke walked right into it."

Lepke met columnist Walter Winchell, the intermediary throughout the negotiations, in a waiting car before being formally introduced to FBI Director J. Edgar Hoover. The plan made the news in grand fashion. Though little was ever mentioned regarding anyone else present at the surrender (besides lots of police), Rosen stated delivery car carrying Winchell and Lepke was actually driven by the reputed "other" boss of Murder Inc. - Albert "Lord High Executioner" Anastasia.

Burton Turkus

The Assistant District Attorney, dubbed *Mr. Arsenic* (by Buggsy Goldstein in an angry rant to reporter Harry Feeney), addressed the Hillside Masonic Lodge in 1944. It was one of many speaking appearances where he reflected on the Murder Inc. trials and the individuals he met, questioned and prosecuted. He explained a theory that, to him, proved to be a common denominator among all the murderous gangsters he encountered – with one baffling exception.

"They all had killer's eyes."

Turkus used his theory during trials, and it was not limited to just the icepick and gun-wielding "Combination" boys. He saw those "eyes" in even the hottest of hot shot mobsters – Luciano, Legs Diamond and Vincent "Mad Dog" Coll.

"When you look into them... you see no hate, love, fear or courage and you never can tell what your subject is thinking."

Only one set of eyes defied the Turkus theory.

"Never have I looked into such soft, luminous, big brown eyes," Turkus recalled. "His expression was so pathetic that for a moment I thought I was looking into the eyes of a young collie dog."

Burton Turkus was describing Louis "Lepke" Buchalter.

০৪ ৪০

Afterword

During and following the discoveries, accusations, indictments, sentences, and controversies that unfolded in early 1940, even more mysteries presented themselves. As we know, the most prominent murder cases the law could build cases upon were highlighted in the media, and attributed-murderers were sent to the electric chair. There were, however, so many people directly and loosely related to the murder Syndicate, well, years of research and volumes could be written just to cover all the intricacies, backstories and mysteries.

Although a number of witnesses, relatives and associates faded into history with little or no information available thereafter, fortunately a few still made the news, post-Murder Inc. So, to close out this little compendium of mysteries and anecdotes, here is a sampling of "last words" on a handful of characters that existed beyond the media sensation.

Whatever Happened to...?

William "Willie" Shapiro, at the time of his two brother's murders, was the subject of speculation over whether or not he had any real involvement in gang rackets. Later reports insinuated he *was* involved after Irving and Meyer were killed. Regardless, Willie was still a Shapiro and the Murder Inc. crew never forgot about him. Late on the night of July 18, 1934, twenty-two-year-old Sidney Weiss was walking along the banks of Fresh Creek, an inlet on the south shore of Brooklyn, when he happened upon four men dressed in suits. "Hot night, isn't it?" rhetorically one asked Weiss. "Kind of desolate, isn't it?" Cordial greeting, yes, but Weiss realized quickly it was a hint to 'go away,' which he did. Still, curiosity brought the young man back a day later – with a shovel in hand. Weiss dug up the spot where the four mysterious men had been. In the hole – a man's body. Examination of the remains confirmed it was Willie Shapiro. He had been beaten, choked and buried alive.

Jacob "Gurrah" Shapiro, an original *Gorilla Boy* with Lepke in the industrial rackets, was never indicted for any actual Murder Inc. related charges after his surrender in 1938. Instead, he was convicted of extortion and sentenced from 15 to life in Sing Sing prison. He was also very proud of the fact that the press had been unable to snap many photos of him over the years – pictures of him are quite rare. Gurrah suffered from several health ailments, diabetes and a heart problem among them. He died in the prison hospital on June 9, 1947 at age 56.

Frank "Big Boy" Davino was convicted for the 1938 murder of fireman Thomas Hitter, and sentenced to die in Sing Sing. During his appeals, Davino was shuttled to and from court with two of Murder Inc.'s most notorious – Happy Maione and Dasher Abbandando – who were also appealing their death sentences. This incidental occurrence branded him, at least by some reporters, as also being a member of murderous Combination. He wasn't. And in 1941, after seeing over twenty of his fellow death row inmates led to their doom, Davino was granted freedom. Further investigations of the Hitter murder case found there was another man of interest, which led to Davino's release. Upon leaving Sing Sing he stated a desire to enlist in the Army and "enjoy the sunshine." No word on whether he got that wish, but it was unlikely. Davino left prison with a case of Tuberculosis.

Seymour "Blue Jaw" Magoon, the only Irish blood member of Murder Inc., and one of the first to turn state's witness, essentially disappeared after the numerous trials. Reports circulated that in the early 2000's Magoon's remains were discovered in a Nevada desert. However, the only reference to that alleged discovery that this author could find was based on an episode of the fictional television series CSI. On a side note, his mother – Anna Magoon – was one of hundreds of people sought during John Harlan Amen's 1941 probe of shady bond dealings.

Ruth Sewall, the woman who earned headlines for having denied the Murder Inc. boys their cut of her bridge games, and reputedly demanded Seymour Magoon keep his men away from her. Well, she quickly tried to quash that story, because she was indeed known for her bridge games and decided talking to O'Dwyer was not in her best interest. In 1948, Sewall garnered more headlines, only this time in Miami – where she again set up shop with a gambling den. She was arrested several times, cases were drawn out, and last word on Sewall – a judge finally dismissed her and told the arresting officers not to bring her back until they had actual evidence.

Charles "The Bug" Workman, the trigger man who took out Dutch Schultz in 1935, was given a life sentence in 1941 after pleading no defense. The Bug maintained his innocence throughout his incarceration, even volunteered once for a PT boat 'suicide' mission against the Japanese that the government considered recruiting for. After serving twenty-three years in prison and having been denied parole seven times, Workman was finally granted freedom in 1964. He quietly rejoined his wife (who consistently visited him in prison throughout the sentence), his children and grandchildren.

Albert "Tick Tock" Tannenbaum, a top witness for the Murder Inc. prosecutors, disappeared for a while after the major trials ended. But when Jack "The Dandy" Parisi was put on trial in 1950 for the Irving Penn murder, Allie was needed for further testimony. He had been living under the radar down south. The last newsworthy mention of his whereabouts came, ironically, in the same story that detailed Charles "The Bug" Workman's release from prison in 1964. The article stated of Tannenbaum, "Five years ago he was reported selling lamp shades in Atlanta Georgia."

Further reports noted Tannenbaum passed away in 1976 somewhere off the coast of Florida.

Albert "The Mad Hatter" Anastasia, the "other" boss of Murder Inc., made out pretty good during the 1940's. He was never prosecuted, joined the army and kept right on doing mob business - until Senator Estes Kefauver began his roundup of mob affiliates in 1950. The famous Kefauver Hearings called for Anastasia – who tried to squirm out of it with a medical ailment. No dice though. He was indeed questioned. Albert had been very closely allied with Frank Costello and Lucky Luciano over all those years, but by the early fifties – another old pal had become an egregious foe. Vito Genovese was taking over the mafia family once named after Luciano. In due course of mob evolution, Albert Anastasia had made a few mistakes (he was impulsive and used the remnants of Murder Inc. for personal vendettas). Genovese wanted Costello, Anastasia and anyone else from the old guard out of his way. In May of 1957, former boxer and Genovese thug – Vincent "The Chin" Gigante ambushed Costello. The bullet only grazed Costello's head, but convinced him to officially 'retire' from the mob's hierarchy.

The Mad Hatter's last day on Earth came while he was receiving a shave in Manhattan's Park Central Hotel, October 25, 1957. Two gunmen entered, motioned for the barber to leave, and blasted Albert into the netherworld. There were hundreds taken in for questioning over the following years. Among the 'persons of interest' – Meyer Lansky, Frank Erickson, George Uffner, and Liz Renay – a star of burlesque and film, who was known for hanging with and/or love affairs with gangsters. Nobody was ever prosecuted for the murder.

William O'Dwyer, the zealous District Attorney of Kings County had political ambition beyond the days of Murder Inc. He ran for Mayor, lost to Fiorello LaGuardia, and then joined the army. He returned and tried for Mayor again. He won in 1945, but by reelection time – O'Dwyer had come under fire for some political corruption. Notwithstanding the trouble, he moved on to become Ambassador to Mexico. Still, the old ghosts of Murder Inc. haunted him. The early 1950's ushered in the Kefauver Hearings, and O'Dwyer was put under the microscope for several Murder Inc. mishaps and mysteries.

William O'Dwyer was rumored to have been quite friendly with Frank Costello, more like outright accused of it. During the Kefauver Hearing sessions, the former DA had been asked numerous times about Costello, such as 'why' the big time boss was not listed as one of the infamous "Big Six" mob titans. Revelations that O'Dwyer rubbed elbows with Costello were brought up to speed when queries of Albert Anastasia's ability to basically remain clear of any Murder Inc. implications were addressed. The point being made regarded the question of whether or not O'Dwyer's alleged kinship with Frank Costello was a cause for top Murder Inc. witness Abe "Kid Twist" Reles to mysteriously wind up dead while under heavy guard. Some investigators were convinced that if Reles was "pushed" out the sixth story window – somebody was paid to do it –. and Costello was potentially the man with the cash raising funds to arrange it.

Though he admitted to meeting Costello a couple times, he defended his Murder Inc. choices saying, "I never heard Costello's name mentioned in any murder in Brooklyn."

He was questioned as to why Albert Anastasia, the man considered a direct boss of Murder Inc., was never prosecuted. O'Dwyer again defended his decisions as District Attorney by explaining that Reles was the proof and when he went "out the window," his case against Anastasia "Went out the window with him."

William O'Dwyer resigned from Ambassador in 1952. The accusations and scrutiny followed him until his death in 1964.

Anthony "Duke" Maffetore, the first "singer" in William O'Dwyer's choir, was truly the catalyst in the downfall of Murder Inc. He and Abraham "Pretty" Levine received suspended sentences as a reward for their cooperation. Dukey went back to a life of crime. In 1950 he was picked up for car theft in Astoria, but failed to return to court the following March. The absence caused his attorney to consider the possibility he was "taken for a ride" and the police worry he "may end up in a bag." Dukey's brothers, Cosmo and Salvatore, who were also indicted for the car theft, told authorities that Dukey hadn't been in contact with even his own wife and children in some time. Then, in mid-May 1951, a bulldozer digging in New Jersey uncovered a body. Investigators reported the badly decomposed find had an icepick in the heart and was *possibly* the remains of Dukey Maffetore. But again the trail went cold, as the ice-picked corpse was not Maffetore. Police weren't ready to quit the search. Another of Dukey's siblings, Vincent Maffetore, and his wife, were hauled in for questioning by a DA the following month. The couple provided a few leads, admitting Dukey had stayed in their Manhattan apartment for week at some point. Subsequent probing suggested Dukey was indeed alive and well – probably living in Florida. However, in yet another wild twist, it was revealed that Vincent's twenty-one year old wife – Elizabeth Crayton - was actually Dukey's step-daughter!

80 03

Notes

Chapter 2

1. Only a month after Reles gang was arrested
   under the controversial 'consorting' statute,
   a meeting of uppermost racketeers would
   commence, birthing – at least partially some
   believe – the official unification of Italian
   and Jewish gangsters in a new "syndicate"
   of crime and the inauguration of what would
   become infamously known as Murder Inc.
   Nine Jewish mobsters were arrested at the
   Hotel Franconia in Manhattan (owned by the
   late Arnold Rothstein (mentor to several of
   the men arrested). They were: Joseph "Doc
   Stacher" Rosen, Benjamin "Bugsy" Siegel,
   Henry (Harry) Teitelbaum, Louis "Lepke"
   Buchalter, Harry Greenberg, Louis Kravitz,
   Jacob "Gurrah" Shapiro, Philip Kovalich and
   Hyman Holtz. Detectives raided the room
   based on the same statute that was
   intended to hold the Reles gang. In similar
   fashion though, all nine men were
   eventually released, as the presiding judge
   felt the law did not justify arresting the men
   when no criminal act had taken place
   (though he made a point to express his
   personal belief most of the men were indeed
   gangsters). Gangland lore *suggests* the

meeting was led by Benjamin "Bugsy" Siegel
and Louis "Lepke" Buchalter, possibly at the
behest of Meyer Lansky. Besides discussing
various rackets they were all involved in,
the word was to be spread of a new joint
venture with Charles "Lucky" Luciano and
his Italian loyalists. Basis for that possibility
stems from the general consensus that two
assassinations – that of mob bosses Joe
"The Boss" Masseria and Salvatore
Maranzano – were planned by Luciano and
Lansky, carried out by both Italian and
Jewish gunmen earlier in 1931.

2. The gang successfully dispatched Meyer
Shapiro into spirit world just two weeks
after being released by Justice Fawcett.
Meyer's body was discovered in a tenement
building on September 17; bullet wound to
the head. Reles, Maione, Goldstein, Strauss
and Anthony "Tony the Sheik" Carillo were
arrested for the murder, but again – all men
were soon released. A third Shapiro, Willie,
was murdered in 1934.

3. Meyer Shapiro was presumed responsible for
an attempted hit on Reles in 1930. The
drive-by shooting injured Martin Goldstein,
lodged two .45 caliber slugs into Reles' back
and killed George DeFeo. Meyer was also
reputed to have kidnapped, battered and
raped Abe Rele's sweetheart (who later
became his wife) as a message.

4. On a larger scale, the notoriety Reles and
company garnered from their ambition,
success and propensity for violent resolve
had earned admiration from Louis "Lepke"
Buchalter and Jacob "Gurrah" Shapiro (not

related to the Shapiro brothers) – two of the major mob figures in competition with both the Shapiro and Amberg brothers (Joe & Louis Amberg's fate came in 1935). Reles, Maione, Strauss and Goldstein had essentially solidified a new career path in the eyes of Lepke. These guys would be the foundation and privileged members of the national syndicate's *enforcement division*, directly overseen Lepke himself.

Chapter 3

1. Iconic photographer Arthur "Weegee" Fellig, known for capturing stark and provocative images throughout New York City from 1935 to 1946, dubbed himself *"The Official Photographer of Murder Inc."* His common nickname, *Weegee*, was spawned from an uncanny ability to arrive at newsworthy scenes often before police did – as though he used a *Ouija Board*. Many of his pictures, which he sold regularly to newspapers, depicted the arrests, deaths and aftermath of New York City's gangland wars.

Chapter 6

1. Albert "Tick Tock" Tannenbaum's parents owned a resort near Loch Sheldrake, where many patrons came for bootleg liquor and gambling. Albert met Jacob "Gurrah" Shapiro and Harry "Big Greenie" Greenberg in 1925. He was offered a job at $35 a week by the gangsters, which eventually ushered him into the murder-for-hire division.

2. Meier (Meyer) "Mickey" Sycoff is perhaps one of the least known members of the Reles gang/Murder Inc. stool pigeons. Although not the most crucial witness within the DA's protection, his history, specifically in 1935, directly connected him as being in usury/shylock business dealings with Reles Gang members, including Carl "Mutt" Goldstein and George "Whitey" Rudnick. Another lesser discussed witness, Oscar Friedman, was responsible for disposing of Murder Inc.'s stolen cars. He pointed investigators to several junkyards where the parts could be found. Friedman, called "The Poet" for allegedly always reading from a poetry book, later told reporters the book of sonnets had been planted on him. "I can barely even write," he later told reporters. "But I can play poker!"

Chapter 7

1. Deputy Sheriff William Cassell was found responsible for allowing Vito Gurino's numerous jailhouse visits with witness Joe Liberto. Cassell, accused of also being 'chummy' with Gurino, was consequently forced to resign.

Chapter 8

1. Stories circulated that a woman was present with Maffetore and Goldstein when Puggy Feinstein's body was being disposed of. Allegedly, the unnamed woman offered or requested to light the match that set Puggy's corpse afire, and later bragged about the incident. Harry "Pittsburgh Phil"

Strauss's girlfriend – Evelyn Mittelman – was most likely to have been the unidentified female, if the story was true. Mittelman was held as a material witness for a period of time, based on information that convinced Burton Turkus she was much more than a mob moll and knew very detailed inner workings of the murder Combination.

2. In an effort to help Capone and Weiss avoid the electric chair in 1944, statements were filed from Happy Maione's brother Louis and sister, Jennie Daddona. Maione's siblings told authorities that on the eve of Harry's execution, their condemned brother expressly claimed it was he who was the actual shooter in the Joseph Rosen murder. At first, defense counsel - for Weiss especially – was confident their motions based on that information would save their client. However, it was not enough and all convicted were put to death.

Chapter 9

1. There are several listings relating Irving Cohen's film roles on IMDB. Under the name *Jack Gordon* there are two separate entries, same biography, different film resumes for each. Another listing confuses the gangster with famous boxing promoter named Irving Cohen.

2. The "Big Six" was a term police and press used to distinguish the top organized crime figures in the New York vicinity during the 1930s -1950's. However, the member list varied – depending on what law

enforcement or media entity was discussing the topic. Following the murder of Dutch Schultz, Lucky Luciano, Bugsy Siegel, Frank Costello, Jacob Shapiro, Louis Buchalter and John Torrio were labeled as the sextet by some accounts, yet other reports suggested Augie Pisano and Ciro Terranova were leadership. During the Kefauver hearings in the early 1950's, former District Attorney William O'Dwyer named the 'Big Six' as Luciano, Meyer Lansky, Willie Moretti, Joe Adonis, the late Bugsy Siegel, yet implicitly omitted Frank Costello – which brought much scrutiny because O'Dwyer, then-Ambassador to Mexico, was suspected of being quite friendly with Costello over the years.

3. Wanted posters for Jack Drucker stated the $500 reward was for either information leading to the arrest of Drucker *or* the "finding of his body."

4. Clinton Prison, located in Dannemora New York, was nicknamed "Little Siberia" for the miserably-cold winters prisoners endured. Charles "Lucky" Luciano also served time in Clinton Prison.

Chapter 10

1. Sholem "Sol" Bernstein, at first, couldn't be found during William O'Dwyer's search mission for Murder Inc. members. Of course the initial thought from investigators was that Sol met his maker for ditching Bugsy Siegel's mission to assassinate Harry Greenberg. That concern was amplified when authorities in Chicago discovered a

burlap sack containing the severed torso and legs of a man. Police were fairly convinced it was the remains of Bernstein, but later that month Sol appeared alive and well, subsequently placed in protective custody by William O'Dwyer's staff.

2. Beside the Harry Greenberg murder indictment, Siegel was indicted for 'harboring a fugitive' (Buchalter). Abe Reles also testified that he and Bugsy Siegel met with then-fugitive Louis "Lepke" Buchalter in a Brooklyn safe-house. Siegel's alibi was based on documentation he had been in Europe on the date Reles claimed they visited Lepke. Siegel stated in court that he "knew" Lepke because they grew up in the same neighborhood. "As for this guy," Siegel stated of Reles, "I never saw him until he appeared in court, here."

80 03

References

AP. "Drucker Senteced 25 Years to Life." *Corning NY Leader*, May 12, 1944: 2.

—. "Three Take 5th in Bronx Loan shark Probe ." *Daily Press*, October 24, 1963: 7.

—. "Three Take 5th in Bronx Loan Shark Probe." *Daily Press*, October 25, 1963: 7.

—. "New York's Gangdom Gives Up Two Bodies." *Herald-Journal*, November 6, 1935: 1.

—. "Insane Gang Slayer Dies in Hospital." *Niagara Falls Gazette*, April 23, 1957: 3.

—. "Court Upholds Conviction of Three Slayers." *Niagra Falls Gazette*, June 2, 1943: 22.

—. "Murder Inc. Inquiry Bares Jewel Thefts." *Syracuse Herald-Journal*, April 4, 1940: 2.

—. "New Murder Counts Asked." *Syracuse Herald-Journal*, April 16, 1940: 6.

—. "Cohen Freed in Murder Ring Killing." *The Binghamton Press*, June 22, 1940: 8.

—. "Body Slain Man Buried Secretly." *The Evening Independent*, July 20, 1934: 1.

—. "Lepke Executed in Chair at Sing Sing." *The Evening Independent*, March 6, 1944: 5.

—. "Summary Justice for N.Y. Gangsters." *The Lowell Sun*, July 22, 1931: 11.

—. "Seventh Death." *The Miami News*, October 23, 1935: 1.

Berger, Meyer. "The Shy Boss of Bloody Murder Inc. Awaits Death in the Electric Chair." *LIFE*, February 28, 1944: 86-87.

Brooklyn Daily Eagle. "2 of Reles Mob Held as Killers of Joe Amberg." December 4, 1935: 1.

Brooklyn Daily Eagle. "Both Maiones Are Free Again." April 25, 1933: 1.

Brooklyn Daily Eagle. "Buggsy Goldstein Freed by Magistrate." September 1, 1936: 2.

Brooklyn Daily Eagle. "Campaign Talk by McGoldrick Barred on Air." October 28, 1935: 5.

Brooklyn Daily Eagle. "Double Murder is Blamed on Labor Dispute." February 7, 1939: 3.

Brooklyn Daily Eagle. "Fawcett Urges Lash for Racket Gangster." September 11, 1931: 2.

Brooklyn Daily Eagle. "Gang Finally Kills Shapiro." September 17, 1931: 2.

Brooklyn Daily Eagle. "Geoghan Gives Date to Police." October 25, 1935: 3.

Brooklyn Daily Eagle. "Geoghan to Act on 31st Arrest of 'Great Lover'." January 22, 1934: 7.

Brooklyn Daily Eagle. "Geoghan to Act on 31st Arrest of 'Great Lover'." January 22, 1931: 7.

Brooklyn Daily Eagle. "Hope Maione Jailing Ends Intimidation." September 18, 1932: 13.

Brooklyn Daily Eagle. "No Bag Holding by Sabbatino." March 7, 1934: 1.

Brooklyn Daily Eagle. "Police Arrest 8 in Narcotics Raid on Bootblack Shop." May 28, 1932: 5.

Brooklyn Daily Eagle. "Police Hunt Three in Beer Store Fight." February 5, 1934: 7.

Brooklyn Eage. "Gang Tries to Spring Maione." April 1, 1940: 2.

Brooklyn Eagle. "Blames Murder Inc. on Brownsville Slums." April 2, 1940: 22.

Brooklyn Eagle. "D.A. Grills Brother of Duke Maffetore." June 27, 1951: 7.

Brooklyn Eagle. "Eyes Are Key to Soul." April 3, 1945: 10.

Brooklyn Eagle. "Happy Maione's Brother Held as Vagrant." November 11, 1942: 9.

Brooklyn Eagle. "Huge Bank Accounts of Mrs. Gold Studied." May 10, 1939: 2.

Brooklyn Eagle. "Judge Martin Calles Reles 'Yellow Dog' at Trial." June 3, 1940: 9.

Brooklyn Eagle. "Maione, Abbandando Doomed; Last Hope Gone." January 9, 1942: 4.

Brooklyn Eagle. "Mangano Brings 5 From Sing Sing for New Trials." January 13, 1941: 8.

Brooklyn Eagle. "Mrs. Gold Free After Bail Reduction." June 16, 1939: 1.

Brooklyn Eagle. "Murder Inc. Hood Feared Slain on Ride." March 24, 1951: 1.

Brooklyn Eagle. "Nitzberg's Defense Calls Informers 'Varmints'." March 11, 1942: 1.

Brooklyn Eagle. "O'Dwyer Snatched 2 From Gang Death." April 5, 1940: 1.

Brooklyn Eagle. "O'Dwyer Snatched Two From Gang Death." April 5, 1940: 1.

Brooklyn Eagle. "Racket Arrest Tightens Net About Officials."
May 5, 1939: 2.

Brooklyn Eagle. "Toss Out Argument Against Payment to
Killing Witness." April 28, 1942: 18.

Brooklyn Eagle. "Two Democratic Chiefs Scored in Bail
Probe." April 8, 1941: 1.

Burton B. Turkus, Sid Feder. *Murder Inc. The Story of the
Syndicate.* Da Capo Press, 2003.

Cipollini, Christian. *Lucky Luciano: Mysterious Tales of a
Gangland Legend.* Strategic Media Books, 2014.

Court of Appeals Points on Behalf of Defendant Abbandando.
(Court of Appeals of State of New York, January
1941).

Davidson, Alice. "All's Right Now for Wrong Drucker." *New
York Post*, December 28, 1943: 3.

Dubill, Bob. "Dutch Schultz's Killer Free After 23 Years."
Herald Statesman, March 10, 1964: 4.

Eisenberg, Dan, Landau. "Lepke." *The Miami News*, November
6, 1979: 23.

Elmaleh, Edmund. *The Canary Sang but Couldn't Fly: The Fatal
Fall of Abe Reles, the Mobster Who Shattered Murder,
Inc.'s Code of Silence.* Union Square Press, 2009.

Evans, Clifford. "Ears to the Ground." *Brooklyn Daily Eagle*, September 14, 1940: 4.

Fino, Ronald, interview by Christian Cipollini. *Former FBI Operative and Author* (2014).

Garcia, Joaquin "Jack", interview by Christian Cipollini. *Former FBI* (2014).

Gourdine, Michael, interview by Christian Cipollini. *Author* (2014).

Heimer, Mel. "Mere Rumors of New Murder Inc. Frightful." *Buckley Post-Herald*, March 30, 1967: 4.

Hill, Gladwin. "Woman is Only Private Citizen on Record to Have Successfully Defied Murder Inc. Gangsters." *The Niagara Falls Gazette*, October 4, 1940: 34.

Howard, James T. "Scared Gangster Runs to Fr. Quinn." *PM*, September 12, 1940: 8.

INS. "2 Questioned on Siegel in Gang Slaying." *Syracuse Herald-Journal*, August 20, 1940: 23.

—. "Woman's Garb Masks Killer - O' Dwyer's Probe Uncovers Details of Slayings of Plasterers." *The Charleston Gazette*, April 21, 1940: 14.

—. "Woman's Garb Masks Killer." *The Charleston Gazette*, April 21, 1940: 14.

Johnson, Malcolm. "O'Dwyer Names Gang Overlords." *Rome News-Tribune*, March 10, 1951: 1.

Logan, Malcolm. "Slot Machine King of Brooklyn Slain." *New York Evening Post*, September 17, 1931: 1.

Long Island Daily Press. "Murder Inc. Leaders to Die in Chair." May 24, 1940: 14.

MacGregor, Donald. "America: Zoned for Crime." *The Spokesman-Review*, June 30, 1940: 52.

Mahon, Jack. "Reles Story Bared Long Murder List." *Syracuse Herald-Journal*, December 4, 1941: 13.

Morris, William. "The Passing of Mr. Shapiro." *Standard Union*, September 19, 1931: 6.

Musel, Robert. "Woman's Tip Finally Traps Murder Inc." *The Binghamton Press*, March 28, 1940: 1940.

Nash, Arthur. *New York City Gangland.* Arcadia Publishing, 2010.

New York Post. "$2500 Bail is Set for GangsterAfter his Car Kills Woman." November 9, 1937: 3.

New York Post. "2 In Police Lineup in Amberg Killing." December 4, 1935: 1.

New York Post. "2500 Bail is Set for Gangster After His Car Kills Woman." November 9, 1937: 3.

MURDER INC.

New York Post. "A Leaner Gurino Get 20-to-Life." April 7, 1942: 11.

New York Post. "A Leaner Gurino Gets 20-to-Life." April 7, 1942: 11.

New York Post. "Brother Keeps Dapper Phil's Trim Tradition." February 3, 1938: 2.

New York Post. "Reles Killed in Flight." November 12, 1941: 8.

New York Sun. "36 Cops Guard Maione Buriel." February 24, 1942: 12.

O'Brian, Jack. "The Voice of Broadway." *Lebanon Daily News*, July 9, 1975: 46.

Pittsburgh Press. "Women Provide Key to Three Murders." March 22, 1940: 23.

PM. "Five Men Once Convicted of Murder Leave Sing Sing for Retrial." January 14, 1941: 19.

PM. "Migden Cops a Plea, Ends Murder Trial." February 18, 1943: 16.

PM. "The Society of Friends of Abraham Reles." November 19, 1940: 17.

Riesel, Victor. "Bullets Failed, So Mafia Runs Rackets with Ballots." *Buffalo Courier Express*, October 14, 1954: 26.

Standard Union. "Gangster Cure Seen in Court in Lamp Posts." July 22, 1931: 2.

Standard Union. "Shapiro Death Laid to Three Taken in Chase." July 20, 1931: 2.

Syracuse Herald-Journal. "Labor Leader Killing Laid to Murder Inc." March 26, 1940: 14.

The Brooklyn Daily Eagle. "Apology For Attack Wins Him Freedom." March 17, 1942: 18.

The Miami News. "Mrs. Sewall Freed in Beach Court Hearing." September 3, 1948: 1B.

The New York Age. "Court Hold Reles' Aid on Charge of Murdering Garage Worker." December 8, 1934: 1.

The New York Sun. "Davino Freed in Murder Case." November 9, 1942.

The New York Sun. "Gangster Slain by Mistake for Meyer Shapiro." July 11, 1931: 2.

The New York Sun. "Maione Denies Link to Gang." May 21, 1940: 14.

The New York Sun. "Three in Brooklyn Held for Murder." February 2, 1940: 17.

The Pittsburgh Press. "Women Provide Key to Three Murders." March 22, 1940: 23.

The Standard Union. "Gang Roundup Saves Slot Czar."
    September 10, 1931: 16.

The Standard Union. "Meyer Shapiro on Spot; Five Seized as
    Slayers." September 17, 1931: z.

The Standard Union. "Whipping Post for Criminals, Urges
    Fawcett." September 11, 1931: 1.

Turkus, Burton. "Gang Wives' Mystery Roles in Killings." *The
    Pittsburgh Press*, December 13, 1951: 21.

UP. "Alibi is Claimed for Bugsy Siegel." *Brooklyn Daily Eagle*,
    May 26, 1941: 5.

—. "Defense Starts Testimony Today in Murder Inc." *Dunkirk
    Evening Observer*, September 18, 1940: 2.

—. "O'Dwyer Sends Out Call for Zwillman." *Kingston Daily
    Freeman*, April 2, 1940: 1.

—. "2 More Arrested in Shapiro Killing." *New York Evening
    Post*, September 18, 1931: 3.

—. "Man Accused of Three Murders is Under Arrest." *The
    Niagara Falls Gazette*, December 28, 1943: 18.

—. "Murder Ring Members Die in Sing Sing." *Utica Daily
    Press*, February 20, 1942: 22.

Woodward, Daisy. *www.anothermag.com.* January 26, 2012.
    http://www.anothermag.com/current/view/1707/W

eegee_Murder_Is_My_Business (accessed August 28, 2014).

ଓ ଃ